Learning Through Groups: A Trainer's Basic Guide

Philip G. Hanson, Ph.D.

University Associates, Inc.
8517 Production Avenue
P.O. Box 26240
San Diego, California 92126

To Robin, Greg, and Scott—my primary group

Acknowledgments

I would like to acknowledge several people who aided in the preparation of this manuscript. To my current secretary, Alma A. Hurlbert, I would like to express my deep appreciation for her stamina and patience in preparing most of the first and all of the second draft of this book and for her willingness to sacrifice evenings and weekends to meet deadlines.

Reba McCoy, my previous secretary, worked through several typings of much of the original material in preparation for this book and previous publications.

I feel extremely fortunate to have as chief of psychology service, in Houston, Dr. Sidney E. Cleveland. He has been very supportive and helpful in all my attempts at research and writing and in the conducting of training for patients and personnel throughout the VA system.

My gratitude also extends to Dr. Cecil Peck, deputy director of mental health and behavioral sciences at the VA central office, who was instrumental in my involvement and leadership in the TIGER project and in the publication of the TIGER handbooks.

Last, and certainly not least, I would like to acknowledge all the trainers with whom I have worked and, in particular, the NTL Institute for Applied Behavioral Science for my development in—and my enjoyment of—the field of human relations training and group learning. In particular, I owe a debt of gratitude to Lee Bradford, who made my "experiment" possible.

Philip G. Hanson
Houston, Texas
April, 1981

TABLE OF CONTENTS

INTRODUCTION

This book is for change agents—those people who work with individuals, groups, and organizations for the purpose of facilitating learning and change.

Before the late 1940s or early 1950s, the field of group work was relegated primarily to what was then known as the "helping professions." These professions included psychology, psychiatry, and social work. With the emergence of the National Training Laboratories (NTL) and similar organizations, the definition of helping professions broadened considerably and ultimately included the roles of "change agents." These events, in turn, expanded the definition of "helper." The ranks of the traditional helpers (therapists, counselors, consultants, social workers, and nurses) were augmented by managers, supervisors, teachers, administrators, community leaders, and students—all of whom worked with people and groups in professional or community settings.

Concurrently, the group became more than just a setting for therapy; it became a vehicle for learning and changing in a variety of institutions in which training in motivation, decision making, problem solving, conflict management, and leadership was introduced to increase personal and organizational effectiveness. Thus, the notion of living, working, and playing in groups made the goal of becoming a more effective group participant a primary goal for participants in many training programs.

This book attempts to provide an overview of what human relations trainers are trying to do, a rationale for what they do, the types of learning experiences in which participants might be involved, and the kinds of goals that participants can expect to achieve. Considerable attention is given to training content, structural issues, and program components before, during, and after the training event to stress the importance of these items as a basis for sound practice.

The book also emphasizes the importance of theory and provides a bridge between theory and practice. Since the advent of the group movement, there has been a proliferation of so-called trainers who are more intrigued with the excitement of group interaction and personal encounter than with training theory and rationale. Consequently, some of these people appear on the scene with their bags of tricks and proceed to push participants in directions that are more relevant to the trainers' needs than to the group members' learning goals. Hopefully, many of these group leaders (some of whom are quite talented) can be encouraged to back up their training skills with a sound basis in—and a healthy respect for—learning theory and training rationale. In this book, theory, instruments, structured experiences, and unstructured group discussion complement and supplement each other to enhance the learning process.

References occasionally are made in the text to the TIGER Program. This refers to the Veterans Administration's system-wide training program, "Training for Individual and Group Effectiveness and Resourcefulness (TIGER)." This program, of which the author was director, was set up by Dr. Cecil Peck, the deputy director of the VA's Mental Health and Behavioral Sciences Service, Washington, D.C. The program, based at the Houston VA Medical Center, was designed to develop trainers in all VA medical centers and outpatient clinics to train and work with VA personnel who had face-to-face contacts with veterans seeking medical services. A product of this program was the publication by Philip G. Hanson, Rodney R. Baker, Joyce Paris, Richard L. Brown-Burke, Richard Ermalinski, and Quentin E. Dinardo, "Training for Individual and Group Effectiveness and Resourcefulness: A Handbook for Trainers," published in 1977 by the Veterans Administration, Department of Medicine and Surgery, Washington, D.C. This handbook was an enlarged version of a previous handbook by the author, also published by the VA Department of Medicine and Surgery in 1973. The authors of the 1977 handbook constituted the national training-of-trainers staff for the TIGER program. The present volume is completely rewritten to accommodate the general population and to provide a broader sweep of the field of human relations training.

Chapter 1

An Introduction to Experiential Group Learning

A HISTORY OF HUMAN RELATIONS TRAINING

The Beginning: Group Dynamics

Human relations training arose from the study of behavior in small groups (Lewin, 1947), which developed into a wider focus on human interactions in many settings. To understand the latter, then, one first must look at the growth of the study of group dynamics.

The term "dynamics" was borrowed from physics and refers to "the branch of physics dealing with the action of forces on bodies either at rest or in motion" or "the forces, physical or moral, at work in any field" (World Book Dictionary, 1973). The study of "group dynamics," therefore, focuses on the forces operating in a group (the field) that affect individual behavior in that group. It also is concerned with how individual behavior affects the group. For example, one force operating in a group may inhibit people from expressing negative feelings (a group norm). Individuals in the group are, therefore, reluctant to express angry feelings. Another force may be an individual who attempts to dominate the group and assume a leadership role; a consequence of this behavior is that other group members may attack that person. These forces can be analyzed through a variety of methods to determine why some behaviors are reinforced and persist and why some are not reinforced and disappear.

In studying group dynamics, or group processes, the potential for individual group members to learn about their own behavior—as they experience it and also through the eyes of others—becomes apparent. Although it began as an object for study, the group soon became a powerful vehicle through which individuals could learn about themselves. The important shift in focus was from observers (who were external to the group) studying group behavior to the group members (internal to the group) studying themselves. The relevant questions became "how do I influence this group?" (not "how does member X influence the group?") and "How do other group members see my participation?" (not "member Y's participation is low in comparison with that of other group members").

Focus on the Individual

As the emphasis shifted to the individual within the group, the field of human relations training began to emerge. Although group processes were still an important area of study, the primary focus in training was on learning how the individual relates to and interacts with other individuals and with groups, in terms of such things as leadership and influence, handling conflict, expressing feelings, competition and cooperation, problem solving, and increasing awareness of oneself and one's impact on others. This focus provides an opportunity for individuals to "stop the world" and take stock of themselves in a situation (the training laboratory) of relative safety and support. Normal everyday pressures and ground rules are suspended in the training environment, and individuals can build a "society" from scratch based on their examinations of their own values and their views of what constitutes effective social action.

This type of training usually takes place in a workshop setting and involves several small study groups. The task of the group is to create an effective learning unit in which people can examine their own behaviors and interactions and can learn from each other as the group attempts to create order from chaos. Training-staff members facilitate the learning process both through personal and structured interventions, but they do not lead the groups in the traditional sense.

The Laboratory Method

The history of human relations training was largely influenced and advanced by the laboratory method of learning and change. The laboratory approach is an educational method developed primarily by the National Training Laboratories (Benne, Bradford, Gibb, & Lippitt, 1975; Bradford, Gibb, & Benne, 1964). During the summer of 1946, a workshop in intergroup relations was held at the State Teachers College in New Britain, Connecticut, during which the concept of the unstructured self-examining group as an experiential educational tool was "discovered." Feedback from the staff to the group participants about individual and group behavior, together with the experiential learning generated by interpersonal and group activity, appeared to produce more learning and stimulate more interest than did the traditional learning structures (seminars, lectures, etc.) of the program. As a consequence of this program, the first workshop in group development was initiated in Bethel, Maine, in 1947 by the National Training Laboratories in Group Development (later to be incorporated as the NTL Institute for Applied Behavioral Science).

Building on their experiences at the New Britain workshop, the innovators of the first NTL laboratory, Kurt Lewin, Leland Bradford, Kenneth Benne, and Ronald Lippitt, combined the expertise and knowledge that made the "experiment" possible. These backgrounds and competencies included the use of research concepts and methods as an instrument for implementing change, original theories in group dynamics and social change, educational philosophy and psychology, adult education, social psychology, and workshop discussion methods. Their concern was to formulate an approach to learning that was strongly supported by research and theory and that could be readily translated by practitioners into action plans and strategies for dealing with social and community problems. The main thrust of this effort was not just to create a body of knowledge in the area of learning and change as it applies to social systems but also to put this information into *practice*. Research for research's sake was not the primary goal, but, rather, research that had action implications (for clarifying and solving human and social problems) was to be valued more highly. As a consequence, the learning methodology chosen was heavily invested with values consistent with the scientific ethos and democratic principles.

Translating this action-research model into experiential learning, or human relations training, Lewin, Bradford, Benne, and Lippitt developed a "laboratory" in which participants (the investigators) were to identify human and social problems as they emerged in the setting, learn the concepts and skills required to deal with these issues, and collaborate in the problem-solving process. What came out of this experience was a reconfirmation of some old hypotheses about living and working and/or a modified or new set of hypotheses to be tested and evaluated in other settings. The members of the laboratory used each other, then, to test their perceptions of reality. Thus, the concept of the T-group (T for training) came about.

Since 1947, NTL has developed and expanded the concepts of the laboratory method, or laboratory education, from the initial focus on small-group behavior to training professionals in organization and community development as well as individual personal growth. The laboratory approach grew primarily from the T-group methodology and incorporated other experiential learning concepts and events such as simulated and structured experiences, role playing, group problem-solving tasks, and self-expression through a variety of creative activities.[1]

Elements of Human Relations Training

For its learning base, human relations training depends on several elements and conditions: (a) the learner is actively involved in the learning experience (i.e., he or she is not a passive recipient of information); (b) each learner is responsible for his or her own learning; (c) the learning process has an affective (emotional) as well as an intellectual component; (d) much of what is learned is generated by the activities and interactions of the learners; (e) the learner is encouraged to experiment with new ways of behaving or

[1]To describe the wide variety of learning experiences involved in these kinds of workshops, the terms *human relations training* and *experiential learning* will be used throughout this text.

problem solving; (f) the learner abstracts principles, hypotheses, and theories that have some action implications for the learner from his or her experiences; and (g) the learning process usually is facilitated by a trainer or consultant who has a professional background in the behavioral sciences and experiential education.

THE GOALS OF TRAINING

The goals of human relations training may be set prior to the workshop, may be developed at the workshop, or may emerge during the group sessions. The training goals also can relate to several levels: the workshop as a whole, the individual groups, and/or the individual group members. In addition, within the goals described in this section, individuals and/or groups may develop or set their own goals.

Typically, a major portion of an individual's life is spent within small social systems called groups. These groups provide the basic support systems for individual survival and growth. A person's general level of effectiveness, therefore, is dependent on how valued the person feels (or is) by the groups in which he or she holds membership. A primary goal of human relations training, then, is to assist[2] individuals to become more effective group participants.

The secondary goals of training spell out the ways in which the primary goal is accomplished. These goals are:

Developing Physical, Emotional, and Intellectual Awareness of Oneself

The greater the awareness one has of oneself, the more information one has for making choices. Self-awareness includes knowledge of one's values and how these values are acted out in everyday behavior. Two ways in which such awareness can be increased are:

---

[2]The word "assist," rather than the word "help," is used because it implies that the participant is in a role of primary responsibility and is being *assisted* in his or her goals by the trainer, who is in a position of secondary importance (as a facilitator).

1. Learning the effects of one's behavior on others. Recognizing the impact one has on others can increase sensitivity in interpersonal relationships.
2. Learning the effects of the behavior of others on oneself. This goal subsumes being in touch with one's own feelings, attitudes, and beliefs.

Learning How Groups Function and the Consequences of Different Group Actions or Processes

These learnings generally are applicable to all groups because all groups have most processes in common (see the discussion of group processes in Chapter 4). This learning includes awareness of how one affects group processes and is, in turn, affected by these processes.

Learning How Groups Interact with One Another When They Are Competing or Cooperating

This goal focuses on the processes or dynamics that occur between groups when they interface on some issue or problem. The understanding to be obtained here is applicable to many back-home groups, particularly those in which stereotypes of the members of other groups create communication barriers and mutually destructive interactions.

Learning More Effective Ways To Solve Problems

This includes the identification of resources in the group and ways to bring these resources to bear appropriately on group problems. The word "resources" here means not only techniques but also the group members themselves.

The study of problem solving also includes how decisions are made and the effects of these decisions on group members' commitment and involvement.

Learning How To Learn

This goal is basic to all the other goals in that it is a process through which continued personal growth is possible. Learning how to learn is accomplished by (a) a willingness to examine one's values and how they affect one's choices; (b) the assumption of an experimental attitude toward one's own behavior and toward one's problems in living; (c) a willingness to take risks, particularly when the risk involves the potential for greater learning; and (d) the creation of a climate for oneself and others in which learning will be a continuous process.

Experiential Learning Versus the Traditional Classroom Approach

There are several elements in the experiential-learning approach that have more potency for implementing the goals of a training program than does a purely cognitive, classroom approach. While more traditional methods of education, such as lectures, panel discussions, and seminars, assume a passive recipient, the learnings from experiential training emerge from the participants' actual experiences and are processed and conceptualized by both participants and staff.

Creating more effective leaders, problem solvers, communicators, and decision makers involves the learning of skills that are analogous, in some ways, to driving an automobile or playing football. In developing these more physical kinds of skills, one usually finds that reading or lectures may contribute to the *understanding* of the skill but are relatively ineffective in developing the skill itself. A plethora of physical and emotional factors comprise the learning process in addition to the purely intellectual ones. The best way to learn a skill is to experience it and practice it; e.g., one may read about the rules of the road but one learns to drive an automobile by getting behind the steering wheel and operating the vehicle.

Experiential learning frequently is used in conjunction with lectures and reading assignments. For example, rather than just reading or hearing about decision making and/or group action, participants in a training program may be given a problem on which they must reach some agreement as a group. During the resulting discussion, many kinds of decisions are made and these have different kinds of impacts on group members' interactions and involvement. At the end of the activity, the group members process their interactions to learn how decisions were made and how these decisions affected group members' commitments to the final product. At this point cognitive material (theory) may be introduced, which is better understood because of the experience that the members have just been through.

Another element present in experiential learning, but not considered in the lecture method, is the affective component of learning. Feelings and the attitudes and perceptions that they support strongly influence the learning process and determine, to a large extent, how we will use what we learn. For example, events associated with strong positive or negative feelings are remembered for much longer periods of time than those events that were accompanied by neutral or no feelings. Another example can be taken from the author's own experience in working with the police and the members of a community (Bell, Cleveland, Hanson, & O'Connell, 1969). Attitudes and prejudices on both sides colored the perceptions that each group had of the other, thereby creating negative stereotypes. Only through face-to-face confrontation in which both groups were able to test their assumptions about each other, look at the behaviors that supported the stereotypes they had of each other, examine some of the feelings or emotions that supported these stereotypes, and work together in a problem-solving manner were the the two groups able to understand the sources of their conflict. The experiential approach is able to reach the affective resources in individuals and make them available for both personal and professional growth.

The Scientific Attitude

The emphasis that is placed on problem solving and scientific inquiry in the workshop setting deserves special attention. The experiential learning approach places high value on fully utilizing the concepts and methods of the social and behavioral sciences, particularly as they apply to the practical affairs of everyday living. Central to the scientific method are such values as objectivity, integrity, and the pursuit of information relevant to the issues regardless of vested interests and political expediency. As a result, decison making and problem solving can be accomplished on the basis of objective evidence. Even the term "laboratory" carries scientific implications and suggests experimental inquiry and scientific methodology (Benne, Bradford, & Lippitt, 1964). Participants directly or indirectly perceive that they all are scientists in that they observe behavior and develop assumptions and hypotheses about people and life. Because they are untrained scientists, however, their biases and prejudices distort their picture of reality and they continuously fall short of testing their assumptions. In the training environment, participants are encouraged to test their assumptions about other group members rather than merely to assume that they are true.

Because scientists have the moral obligation to consider all the facts in any problem situation, the person who is trying to make life a science must remember that other people's feelings are facts. In the human-relations laboratory, the attitudes and feelings of others must be taken into consideration and weighed with as much respect as one accords to any other data. The human facts revealed then become available for improved theory construction and more realistic choices.

Some participants arrive at a training event with narrow or unsatisfying ways of experiencing life and handling life's dilemmas. Despite the fact that their typical (fight-flight) responses have frequently not been very effective, they continue to repeat them. One of the goals of human relations training is to break up this pattern and to create space for people to experience and do things differently. The idea of the participant being involved in scientific inquiry and experimentation helps to promote an atmosphere of flexibility.

Problem Solving

Problem-solving behaviors are facilitated by means of planned activities and group discussions in which participants discover that there are many different perceptions of a problem and many alternative solutions. Basic problem-solving techniques, such as the dilemma-invention-feedback-generalization (DIFG) formula (Blake & Mouton, 1961, 1962), and Lewin's (1947) force-field analysis (FFA) can be presented as cognitive background and then experienced in an actual problem-solving activity. In the DIFG activity, participants are asked to state a dilemma, describe their typical ways to handle the dilemma, anticipate the kind of feedback these methods would generate, and abstract some principles that could be applied in a similar situation. When these items are collected, summarized, and discussed, it becomes obvious that the one problem situation may be seen from many different angles and that many alternative solutions can be offered.

In the force-field approach, individuals also may select an actual problem from an ongoing group and analyze all the forces *for* (driving force) and *against* (restraining force) changing the situation. A plan of action then may be outlined by the group to assist it in altering these forces to resolve the problem. Both of these problem-solving approaches can be used repeatedly for dilemmas that arise in the workshop and for problems in the back-home setting.

THE PHILOSOPHICAL BASIS OF HUMAN RELATIONS TRAINING

Individual Needs

People are basically self-motivated and cooperative, and they need to work and live in systems that respect them and their humanity. People also will support what they help to create. Individuals will have more investment in and commitment to a venture or project if they participate in making decisions and in solving problems, particularly if the results affect their lives at home, in the community, or at work.

People have growth needs that develop from infancy to maturity. Along the way, people change from being passive to being active, dependent to independent; their behaviors change from simple to complex, their perspectives from short-term to long-term, and their status from subordinate to equal or superordinate. In addition, people grow in self-awareness and control over themselves (Argyris, 1957). Growth needs are activated by a certain amount of psychological energy that exists in all individuals and will find some kind of expression even when the needs are unmet. When not blocked or thwarted by community or organizational practices or norms that inhibit them, these predispositions toward growth will facilitate the development of healthy, mature, and self-actualizing individuals.

Values

The values supporting human interaction training can be categorized into three major concerns: scientific inquiry, the democratic process, and the helping relationship. A basic value in which all other values are embedded is embodied by the terms "humanism" and "human rights." This value is reflected in Kant's Categorical Imperative (Durant, 1954): "Act as if the maxim of our action were to become by our will a universal law of nature . . . . So act as to treat humanity, whether in thine own person or in that of another, in every case as an end, never only as a means." Essentially, the humanistic value mandates that we guide our behaviors in a way that does not discount, diminish, or dehumanize any person or group, In this world of constant crises, the humanistic prescription is extremely difficult to live by and is, at the same time, our only hope.

The Democratic Process

In many organizations, people often are remote from the decisions that affect their lives. The remoteness removes them from the responsibility for managing many aspects of their own lives. Many individuals lapse into passivity, lose enthusiasm, and abdicate participation in planning and executing personal goals.

The democratic process fosters responsible involvement in decision making in regard to the affairs that concern one's own work and life. The process also involves a commitment to confront problems with an objective, problem-solving attitude, to collaborate with others in defining problems, and to work through solutions. This implies testing one's own assumptions, biases, and values as they impinge on the problem-solving process. The democratic process also implies valuing evidence that is objective and relevant to the issues rather than maintaining personal or political points of view that are refuted by the data.

Participants in a training workshop must feel that they have the power to change their behaviors and to assume full responsibility for these changes and for the consequences.

The job of the workshop staff is to create a climate that encourages self-expression and makes it possible for the participants to recognize and develop their own assets and feel that they have something of value to contribute. This allows participants to become part of creative and decision-making processes of their own design (Johnson & Hanson, 1979). In other words, the focus is on internal rather than external control and the task is one of freeing the participants to realize their potential and "to become more capable and less dependent" (Bradford, 1961).

Helping Relationships

The keynote of group democratic action is collaboration in making decisions, in providing helpful feedback, in assisting others to express themselves, in giving emotional support and acceptance, in dealing more effectively with conflict and change, and in improving the helping process itself. Group members must become cooperatively interdependent. Each participant should provide the kind of assistance that he or she is most qualified to give and should recieve the assistance that is most appropriate to his or her needs. As groups develop interpersonal trust and confidence, the need for help is expressed more openly. Participants begin to realize that helping relationships are most effective and satisfying when the assistance offered does not encourage dependency but enables the receivers to work out solutions for themselves. In this way participants develop more confidence in their ability to cope with problems. They become more capable of contributing something worthwhile to the group and to the training program.

To best help each other, participants should be aware of different styles of helping and their consequences. They also must be aware of the barriers to and difficulties of both giving and receiving help. An analysis of helping relationships can be made to introduce the different purposes of seeking help and the kinds of communication involved in each helping situation. The expectations of helper and receiver also are examined and discussed by means of structured activities and theory sessions or can be focused as the subject arises spontaneously in the group.

ETHICS IN TRAINING

Clearly Stated Goals

People attend workshops or training events in order to achieve certain goals. They expect the trainers to facilitate the achievement of these goals by using their specialized skills. The trainers then consciously create a training situation to help the participants realize their goals. The question of ethics arises when trainers use their skills to move participants in a direction that violates the participants' values or goals or produces changes they do not want. Many of the methods used in experiential learning can have considerable impact on the participants and, therefore, may be met with resistance. Resistance to a method, however, should not be confused with resistance to a goal. The trainer can help participants to move through resistance to learning and change, but if the learning goal is *not* what the participants want or violates their values, their right to choose *not* to change should be respected. The learning goals and methods to be used in a training workshop should be clearly stated so that participants have as clear a picture as possible of what they are "buying." This does not mean that each element of the training design must be described, but the major vehicles through which learning takes place should be cited. For example, if plenary sessions, structured activities, and small group meetings are the primary modes of learning, this may be stated in the workshop brochure.

Of course, the trainers must clarify the purposes of the workshop for themselves. This clarification provides guidelines for what interventions are or are not appropriate in the workshop and what the values will be regarding trainer and participant behavior. This clarification is then checked for congruency with workshop goals as described in the brochure. It is extremely disconcerting to participants to arrive at a workshop expecting one thing and to experience something entirely different.

In many cases, people arrive at workshops having received no prior information at all. Managers or executives from a variety of organizations often decide what their subordinates need and send them to a particular workshop to obtain "it." The task for the workshop staff is then to bring these participants "on board" by clarifying their areas of confusion and legitimizing their mixed feelings.

Voluntarism Versus Coercion

Closely related to the issue of participant expectations is the problem of those who were coerced, directly or indirectly, into attending. Ideally, for participants to benefit most from an experiential learning situation, they should not only know what to expect but also *want* to experience it. If the primary value underlying human relations training is the democratic process, to coerce people into attending a workshop violates this value. Whether the coercion be direct or subtle, when participants arrive at a workshop under this condition, their feelings of resentment and resistance must be dealt with before learning can occur.

The staff must attend to feelings of resistance immediately, before they affect other participants or block a potential learning experience. The way to deal with these feelings is to surface them and legitimize their validity for discussion. Once the resistant participants have described their feelings, they can be faced with the fact that they *are* in the training group, regardless of how they got there, and that they have only two real options (leaving the workshop is not a real option since the participants usually were "sent" or are quite far from home). The first option is to resist the workshop by not participating, not becoming involved, and assuming a detached (or sabotaging) role in the group. The second option is to assume the following attitude: "I'm here; I'm angry and resentful, but I'm here. These people (the group) are not responsible for my predicament. What sense does it make to fight them? Since I am here and will be here for [a week, three days, etc.], how can I best use this time? What can I learn for myself and how can I contribute to this group?" In most cases, presenting these options, while at the same time supporting the participants' negative feelings as legitimate, reduces their resistance and, at best, shifts their attitude to that of "Well, I'll give it a try."

Training Versus Therapy

Experiential learning, with its focus on the affective components of behavior, is sometimes utilized by people with personal problems for the purpose of obtaining "bootleg therapy." What creates confusion is that some training goals and the goals of therapy are the same, i.e., greater self-awareness and interpersonal competence. In therapy, the client comes for help because of some perceived inadequacy and the treatment is remedial in nature. In training, participants are assumed to be functioning adequately or competently, but want to *increase* their competence, e.g., become better teachers, managers, or therapists. There is considerable overlap among all learning or growth processes; this can be illustrated by a continuum from classroom→seminar→topic (task) group→structured, experiential workshop→T-group → personal-growth group→therapy.

In group therapy, sessions may be conducted with little or no attention to group process. In contrast, one of the primary functions of the training group is to study its own process. The training group is a miniature social system in which group members must surface and move from one process issue to another; thus, process issues surrounding leadership, decision making, task and maintenance functions, norms setting, and conflict management are dealt with as they emerge in the group.

Human relations training focuses almost completely on here-and-now experiences with some back-home application, but there is no one-to-one, in-depth exploration of back-home personal problems. While many therapists also focus on here-and-now experiences, the reference point of the experience may be historical or a current there-and-then crisis. In other words, back-home personal problems are seen as grist for the mill in therapy groups but are not appropriate material in training groups.

In training, if participants begin to move in the direction of therapy, the trainer will refocus their attention to the here-and-now group and its goals. This is not to imply that much of what a person learns in a workshop is not applicable or relevant to back-home personal problems; many of the insights gained in a workshop experience can be transferred to family and work life.

It is always a painful and anxiety-producing experience when a group member behaves in a way that is not functional to his or her own learning or to the group's learning. As rare as this event is in any groups that are conducted by professional trainers, it is even more rare in structured workshops, because the structure itself provides safety. In the training group, a supportive and stabilizing resource is the willingness of most group members to both help and support a fellow participant who is in distress.

Milder forms of this kind of problem frequently can be handled by the group and group leader, who provide support and acceptance without allowing the individual to immobilize the group. More seriously disturbed individuals, however, may have to be removed from the group by the trainers and encouraged to seek competent therapeutic help. In these situations, it is clearly the responsibility of the trainer, not the group, to handle the member in distress. Participants pay for what they expect to learn, and this does not include dealing with the trauma of an individual in serious trouble. Trainers need to use their own judgment and obtain psychiatric consultation if it is available. If it is not available, the trainers need to work with the individual (on an individual basis) to obtain the necessary referral and to assist that person to leave the workshop. Individuals in distress may have all kinds of feelings about leaving the group and need the support of both the trainer and the group to convince them that the decision comes from a position of strength rather than one of weakness. The group also may need subsequent support and will have to work through its own feelings (e.g., guilt, anxiety, sense of loss) about the loss of the distressed individual. Encouraging participants to accept the help they need may be a successful outcome of a human-relations training experience, rather than a failure.

NORMS

At the beginning of the training event, the participants should be apprised of what will occur during the training event and of certain norms or ground rules that will be encouraged and reinforced throughout the life of the group and the training program. These norms are typical of almost all human relations training approaches.

Participation

Because the democratic process implies participation, involvement, and commitment, each individual needs to participate in decisions that affect group goals, feel responsibility to and ownership of the group's task, experience a sense of contribution, and be acknowledged for that contribution. People support what they help to create.

Participation is also a necessary ingredient in the process of learning about oneself. Obviously, for behavior to be discussed, examined, or rewarded, it must first occur. Inactive and silent members offer very little material with which the group can work and to which it can react. These members must be drawn into the group by some means.

Gatekeeping, for example, is a skill that facilitates equal distribution of participation; the function can be assumed by any member. It is a simple technique, primarily for bringing silent members into group action; sometimes it can be used to equalize participation when there are overly dominant group members. (Rothaus, Johnson, & Lyle, 1964). In short, it is the function of "opening the gate" for members who are reticent or unsure of themselves or their commitment to participate. This can be done merely by saying something such as "We haven't heard from you yet, Tom; what do you think?" The gatekeeping function can be introduced and practiced by means of a structured activity or it can be assigned openly to members of the group and modeled by the training staff.

Participation itself, however, is not sufficient to insure group growth, cohesion, or democratic action. High individual participation may signify highly autocratic and controlling behavior in which decisions may be imposed on the group rather than shared, struggles for leadership may occur, and anxious members may turn group meetings into rap sessions or withdraw in the face of conflict. Thus, influential members may manipulate the group and lead it into unproductive channels. Channels of communication then may close, sealing up tension and anxiety and disintegrating group cohesion. In contrast, another style of participation may create a group climate that is conducive to open, free expression and an eagerness to get things done.

Examination of participation styles and their effect on group action can be implemented through the development of group process skills and feedback on leadership style. For example, the value and effects of democratic, autocratic, and laissez faire styles of leadership behavior can be evaluated throughout the laboratory experience in terms of the situational determinants and the individual's personal makeup.

Shared Responsibility

Placing responsibility for group action in the hands of the participants may appear to relieve the staff of some responsibility. Sometimes, however, the staff may find itself in a double bind when participants make decisions that staff members feel are not the most effective. Staff members then must exert influence in ways that are not autocratic or perceived as arbitrary. It is important, therefore, that staff members be present when decisions are being made by and for the workshop community. In times of crisis, the easiest, least anxiety-provoking, and most enticing solution usually is for the staff to design a format that will allow the participants to work out the problem.

The issue of shared responsibility, it should be noted, is dependent on the level of skill of the participants. Staff members will take primary responsibility for designing the workshop experience—particularly the early phases. Later, when the participants have developed the relevant skills, the staff may share this responsibility or even turn over parts of the program to the participants to assess or design their own learning experience. The democracy evidenced in many workshops lies in the trainers' values about human beings, as reflected in the philosophy of human interaction training, not in its methodology. The methods are valued primarily because they facilitate goal achievement.

Openness and Risk Taking

Most people attempt to organize their lives in ways that will maximize comfort and familiarity, regularity and predictability, habit and precedent. They also attempt to minimize forces that could disrupt these patterns. Most individuals attempt to build relationships that are mutually supportive and in which their expectations about themselves and other people are met. As long as expectations are met, people are predictable and their level of comfort is high. When expectations are not met (however unrealistic they may be), people become less predictable and more insecure.

Groups handle the problem of security by establishing ground rules and instituting standards of behavior for group members. The members bring with them attitudes, values, needs, and expectations that influence the dimensions along which the group will operate. Any perceived deviation from the norms to which the group subscribes will generate resistance. For example, a norm against confrontation or dealing with conflict may exist in a group. So, when the atmosphere of the group is tense, the members may act as if the tension is not present by avoiding or changing the subject, attempting to be humorous, or calling for a break period. The members fear that by surfacing the conflict, they will lose control of their feelings and relationships will be disrupted beyond repair. This risk must be faced, however, if the group and the individuals in it are to continue to grow and mature.

The group can progress only when individuals are willing to take some risks and to support and encourage others to do the same. In order to explore the impact of one person's behavior on others and vice versa, participants must expose their feelings, perceptions, and attitudes to one another in a feedback process. The paradox is that a climate of trust and openness must be developed before most members are willing to take risks, but in order to develop this climate, some risk taking must first occur.

In the process of developing a climate of openness, people frequently press others to be open and take risks without first exposing their own thoughts and feelings. It is helpful at this stage for the trainer to model the desired behavior by sharing his or her own feelings and perceptions with the group. This usually encourages others to be open.

There is a "false" openness that is destructive, and this should be discouraged and dealt with when it occurs. In this maneuver, one member "lays it on" another member, the trainer, or the group in the guise of openness. This process frequently is described as "the helper strikes again."

Unstructured trainer interventions and experiential activities can facilitate the opening-up process. It is important, however, to graduate this process in terms of the participants' needs, rather than in terms of the trainer's needs. Moving participants too rapidly into activities that involve interpersonal risk taking and self-exposure can be extremely threatening and can create strong feelings of discomfort and resistance. On the other hand, moving too slowly can create feelings of inertia, boredom, and frustration.

The relationship between openness and risk taking is very subtle and highly individualized. What threatens one individual may be completely neutral for another. Furthermore, the levels of openness and risk taking displayed by two individuals may appear to be the same, but the actual level of threat experienced internally by the two people may be quite different. Events in the group also can facilitate or inhibit openness and risk taking. Generally, if the group members are working to build a climate of trust, increased openness, risk taking, and the potential for greater learning will result. The problem for the trainer and the group members is one of sensitivity and timing, i.e., obtaining a balance between providing necessary safety for group members and pushing the limits of that safety for individual growth and effective group functioning.

Reality as Experience in the Process of Change

In talking about change, one must address the problem of reality. There are two kinds of reality: one is through agreement and the other is experience. The reality that exists externally to us is the one that is reached through agreement (social reality). That is, we agree that a chair is a chair and a table is a table. We agree on what is wrong and what is right, good or bad, legal or illegal, ugly or beautiful. It is this kind of reality that enables us to communicate with others and to function in society.

The second kind of reality is one's own personal experience, which one creates for oneself. The way each person experiences events and the way those events are perceived and interpreted is peculiar to each individual. Although external events may trigger feelings, attitudes, and memories of previous experiences that affect or color the present experience, such *reactions* all come from *within* the individual. Therefore, each person's experience—even of the same event—will be different from other people's. As Kant pointed out over two hundred years ago, you never can know the "thing in itself." Human beings do not passively receive external stimuli; they sort, select, and interpret perceptions before choosing a response (whether consciously or unconsciously). Therefore, no thought, action, or other stimulus can be experienced directly or "purely."

The problem that arises from this diversity of experience is the question of whose reality is real. We are inclined to apply the same kind of reasoning in considering the reality "out there" as that which we use in relation to our own experience. As a consequence, people frequently argue about whose experience is correct without realizing that their reasoning is not appropriate. In fact, the most individuals can say is that they experience something differently or similarly. One cannot say that one's own reality is "right" and another's is "wrong." Reality, after all, is only a point of view.

The trainer can help participants to be aware of what they are experiencing at any given moment by focusing their attention on their present feelings, sensations, perceptions, thoughts, images, and attitudes. This frequently is referred to as "getting into the experience"; it includes noticing what is happening in one's body and what feelings, thoughts, and images are emerging into aware-ness. The experience is avoided or negated if one tries to evaluate it, to make sense of it, or to assign a cause-and-effect relationship to it. The skill is just to notice what is happening and accept whatever it is.

People frequently try to avoid or suppress (resist) unpleasant experiences in order to be rid of them. When we resist an experience, it persists. Completing an experience, however, leaves an empty space in which we can create another experience. If the remnants of a previous experience persist, they interfere with the new experience. Completing an experience facilitates the change process.

Equal Vulnerability

Another norm is that of equal vulnerability, which means that all involved participants are equally vulnerable in the experience unless all have agreed otherwise. Because of this norm, it is a mistake to allow floating participant-observers or roving guests in the workshop, even if they are sponsors of the event. The one exception to the equal-vulnerability norm is, in some respects, the trainer.

The norm of equal vulnerability operates in an equally important way during specific activities. For example, in the classic group-on-group observation activity, the outside (observer) group changes places with the inner (observed) group. Failure to reverse these observer and participant roles would violate the norm of equal vulnerability and probably would create "bad feelings" within the total group. For example, in one workshop the participants—with the best of intentions—designed an activity in which four participants were given the task of observing four groups meeting separately within the community. The observers' task was to report what they observed about the four groups to the total community. It is no wonder that this type of observer-diagnosing-reporting design is known as "lynching." The four observers were astounded when their comments were met with both hostility and rejection.

Staying in the "Here-and-Now"

In most training groups, an additional norm is the restriction on "there-and-then" content, i.e., past experiences or back-home problems. Members are urged to keep the focus on current content. In this way the group avoids becoming bogged down in any member's back-home problems, and the members are forced to assume responsibility for what they are doing or saying at that time, rather than being allowed to focus on issues in the past to justify their attitudes or actions. Of course, this does not preclude the application of new learnings or techniques to back-home problems and the discussion of how this application can best be accomplished.

REFERENCES

Argyris, C. *Personality and organization*. New York: Harper & Row, 1957.

Bell, R.L., Cleveland, S.E., Hanson, P.G., & O'Connell, W.E. Small-group dialogue and discussion: An approach to police-community relationships. *The Journal of Criminal Law, Criminology and Police Science*, 1969, *60*(2), 242-246.

Benne, K.D., Bradford, L.P., Gibb, J.R., & Lippitt, R.O. (Eds.). *The laboratory method of changing and learning: Theory and application*. Palo Alto, CA: Science & Behavior Books, 1975.

Blake, R.R., & Mouton, J.S. *Group dynamics: Key to decision making*. Houston, TX: Gulf, 1961.

Blake, R.R., & Mouton, J.S. The instrumented training laboratory. *Issues in human relations training*, 1962, *5*, 61-76.

Bradford, L.P. A fundamental of democracy. In R. Lippitt (Ed.), *Leadership in action*. Arlington, VA: National Training Laboratories (Selected Reading Series 2), 1961.

Bradford, L.P., Gibb, J.R., & Benne, K.D. (Eds.). *T-group theory and laboratory method*. New York: John Wiley, 1964.

Durant, W. *The story of philosophy: The lives and opinions of the greater philosophers*. New York: Pocket Books, 1954.

Johnson, D.L., & Hanson, P.G. Locus of control and behavior in treatment groups. *Journal of Personality Assessment*, 1979, *43*(2), 177-183.

Lewin, K. Frontiers in group dynamics: I. Concept, method, and reality in social sciences: Social equilibria and social change. *Human Relations*, 1947, *1*(1), 5-41.

Rothaus, P., Johnson, D.L., & Lyle, F.A. Group participation training for psychiatric patients. *Journal of Counseling Psychology*, 1964, *11*(3), 230-239.

World book dictionary. New York: Doubleday, 1973.

Chapter 2

Learning and Change

THE LEARNING PROCESS

Motivation

Very little change occurs in an individual unless he or she is motivated and ready to change. When dealing with highly personal and often ingrained attitudes of individuals about themselves, any suggestion of a need for change can be threatening to people's feelings of security about themselves and their life styles. In part, the problem of motivation to change is solved when individuals choose to come to a training program. For those individuals who are "sent" for training, the problem of motivation is more crucial. Their feelings of resistance need to be legitimized and accepted and their attitudes about being in the training setting must be surfaced and handled early in the process. Otherwise, their continued resistance can become a chronic problem for the group.

Once in the program, a member's willingness to change also can be increased by the social influence of the group, particularly when the group has a democratic, participative atmosphere. Bovard (1953), for example, has shown that peer groups open up individuals to interpersonal influence.

Perceived Relevance of the Training Program to the Participants' Needs

The learning process begins when the prospective participants begin to collect information about the training program, generally through reading and by talking to previous participants. Through these processes, they assess the match between their own needs and the potential learnings from the program. For this reason, it is important that the training program and its goals be clearly explained in the advertising literature, informational brochures, or in personal contacts. Unless applicants perceive the program as appropriate to their own needs and as having the potential for moving them in the directions in which they want to go, motivation to change will be minimal. Once they enter the program, and questions of motivation and relevance have been resolved, participants immediately become involved in a process of change that is characterized by three major phases: *unfreezing, change,* and *refreezing* (Lewin, 1947).

Unfreezing

Unless the participants have benefited from a considerable amount of previous training experience, they are in a "frozen" state in terms of openness to learning. In other words, unexamined attitudes and habitual modes of response are intact, and perceptions of self and others are relatively fixed. Before change can take place, the participants must go through a process of unfreezing their typical attitudes and behaviors. This process can be very threatening to the individual, and resistance can be expected. In order for unfreezing to take place, the supports for the old attitudes must be surfaced and examined and experimentation and risk taking must be encouraged. Furthermore, any change in the desired direction should be supported by the group.

The unfreezing process is further implemented when the participants are forced to look at themselves in ways they might not have considered previously. The back-home status of members usually is not recognized or acknowledged in the egalitarian training atmosphere, and the de-emphasis of the traditionally authoritarian role of the professional staff soon becomes apparent. The program is characterized by informality, the absence of direction by the "authority," and the expectation that participants are primarily responsible for their own learnings; all of this makes it difficult for participants to fall back on their previously learned role behaviors. Furthermore, the reduction of privacy in everyday activities, the sharing of facilities, and the lack of structure in the small groups creates a unique situation for which many of the members' repertoires of responses are not adequate.

The atmosphere of the training workshop is saturated with new attitudes that emphasize the value of experimentation in a climate that supports self-examination and reduces the risk of trying out new responses. Total involvement in the program, along with peers who are going through the same process and experiencing the same anxieties, reduces the threat in the situation. The norms of this new culture, in fact, make "changing" desirable, rather than a sign of weakness or failure.

Thus, participants become part of a miniature society that is quite different from the ones they have just left (Blake, Mouton, & Blansfield, 1961). Habitual styles of behavior and stereotypical attitudes no longer seem appropriate. New norms replace the old. Standards are developed that reward individuals for being accepting and permissive, for giving reassurance and assistance, for changing attitudes and behaviors in more effective directions, and for experimenting with new responses. A key factor in the success of this environment is that expectations are different. Participants expect one another to talk about personal issues and concerns and about heretofore taboo subjects. Value is placed on expressing and sensing feelings. As the unfreezing process takes place, the participants discover new and more effective ways (concepts and skills) of coping with their present situations.

Changing

Involvement

Genuine learning and change require that participants be involved personally in the group, have an emotional investment in it, and share its responsibilities. The group must be attractive and rewarding enough so that participants will allow others to influence them and will influence others in return. As the training program progresses, the group becomes increasingly cohesive and the fears and anxieties about changing are progressively reduced. As the participants develop more trust in each other, they discover that failure is not unforgivable, the consequences of failure are not tragic, and the rewards of taking risks are satisfying.

Levels of Learning

The laboratory training method utilizes personal experience on two levels of learning: feeling and intellect. Much of the language of feeling is developed by examining one's experiences with others during analyses of group processes and group members' inter-actions. By assuming the dual role of participant and observer, group members examine their own and others' feelings and reactions as they participate in group activities. To aid the development of sensitivity at the feeling level, the underlying concepts of effective participant behavior frequently are presented in cognitive terms during theory sessions and are surfaced and reinforced by partici-pants and trainers during group meetings. A considerable amount of information is given and is available to participants in the form of lectures, exercises, problem-solving sessions, role plays, handouts, and informal group discussions both during and between group sessions. Rating sheets and behavioral scales also can be used to focus attention on the participants' feelings and reactions and on important aspects of group dynamics. (The specific uses of these techniques are discussed in Chapter 5.)

Kinds of Learning

Two primary kinds of learning can be identified in the change process: action learning and process learning. The first involves the learning of skills—how to *act* or *react* in particular situations. These may include how to resolve conflict productively when it arises in the group, how to include the silent members, when to summarize, how to clarify goals, and how to give feedback constructively. The second kind of learning, process learning, is accomplished most readily by taking an experimental, diagnostic approach to *under-standing* one's own behavior and the behavior of others in groups and by focusing attention on feelings and attitudes. Crucial in process learning is the development of the role of participant-observer-learner, in which each participant actively involves himself in the group, observes and is interested in his own and others' feelings and reactions, and tries to derive meaning from his experiences by abstracting basic principles of effective interpersonal behavior. Most important, perhaps, is that each participant learn how to create a climate of trust in relationships; such a climate enables a person to continue to learn and grow personally after leaving the training program.

Mechanisms for Learning

Two mechanisms in the learning process, identification and internalization, influence the participants to change and assist them in assuming the multiple role of participant-observer-learner (Schein, 1962). In the first, participants learn new attitudes by identifying with and imitating one or more models in the social environment— either another group participant or a staff member. An open, inquiring, experimental life style is repeatedly suggested and demonstrated by highly visible staff members and in informal group sessions. The staff members must exemplify, in their relationships with one another and with the participants, the philosophy of the program. Anything else would be seen as hypocrisy.

The second mechanism, internalization, occurs when participants confront unavoidable problem situations in the laboratory for which they have no adequate coping behaviors. When old approaches and the attitudes behind these approaches are ineffective, participants are forced to develop new approaches to resolve the problems effectively. Whether or not these new attitudes will be adopted depends on whether or not the participants experience the new attitudes and the resultant behaviors as being really useful to them. These changes, in turn, will be reinforced if the group's interactions demonstrate the lack of utility or the negative consequences of the old attitudes and behaviors and support the new attitudes and behaviors.

Focuses of Learning

Participants in training can move in two useful directions: toward a better understanding of the group in process and toward a better understanding of the self in process (Wechsler, Massarik, & Tannenbaum, 1962). In most groups, both directions are taken and the focus of attention shifts back and forth. The first, understanding group processes, includes the development of skills and sensitivity in observing, analyzing, and discussing one's own group in action. Such scrutiny deepens the understanding of group problem solving, group decision making, and the complex forces that determine group behavior. What is learned about group norms, group functions, or group cohesion and growth, for example, will be instrumental in promoting effective participation in other social groups after the laboratory experience.

The other direction, understanding of self in process, enables participants to become more aware of their own feelings and to understand the nature of these feelings as they struggle to create places for themselves in a relatively unstructured group. In this highly provocative setting, group members must learn how to give and accept influence, manage their anxiety and hostility, express and receive affection, deal with feelings of loneliness and alienation, and test their own interpersonal competency. In a climate of trust, the participants can begin to know themselves more intimately and objectively through a willingness to take risks (expose their thoughts and feelings) and through the feedback provided by other group members. Because their relationships in the group are genuine samples of themselves in action, participants can gain a better understanding of all their relationships.

To implement change, a minimum of seven to nine hours a day, every day, for a period of a few days to two weeks is spent in exposing participants to the social phenomenon of a developing group. By increasing their sensitivity and sharpening their ability to act effectively and satisfyingly in relation to others; by developing sophistication in observing, describing, and analyzing ineffective and effective interpersonal and group behaviors, the participants begin to use the concepts of behavioral science to examine both real and simulated problem situations. These concepts also emerge and are made explicit from ongoing, unstructured, group sessions. Members are encouraged to analyze their own group processes and are given conceptual tools to do this more effectively. Rating scales and feedback instruments also may be used to focus the members' attention on important aspects of individual and group behavior; they also help members to check their self-perceptions against those of other members. When no specific structure or direction is given to the group, the members are forced to fall back on their own resources and to assume functions that usually are ascribed to a more traditional group leader. This, in itself, may be a significant change in social behavior.

Refreezing

Refreezing describes the process by which the new attitudes and behaviors acquired during the changing phase are integrated into the participants' ongoing significant relationships and personal makeup. The term "integration" better describes the process and avoids the connotation that behaviors are frozen again. Lewin himself did not intend this connotation and saw refreezing as a temporary state subject to change again as the situation changed and the learned behaviors were no longer adequate to meet new demands.

The extent to which refreezing is successful depends on the extent to which internalization and identification take place. These, in turn, are dependent on support by others and the reinforcement that occurs when one's attitudes and behaviors lead to more satisfying and effective interpersonal relationships and a greater sense of awareness and well-being. Positive feedback from other group members, staff, and back-home people to the newly developed behavioral responses provide the major impetus for continuing those responses. Therefore, to facilitate continued growth, it is important that the participants utilize or develop support systems in their back-home settings.

THE CONCEPT OF CHANGE AS A CONTINUOUS PROCESS

Attitudes About Change

One of the major characteristics of contemporary society is change. Change is a continuous process; it occurs everywhere and in everything. This fluidity creates an atmosphere of temporariness that may be seen as threatening to established social and institutional norms and values. Much change also is perceived as haphazard, out of control, or externally imposed.

A typical response to change is to resist the process by defending or maintaining the status quo. A major problem with this solution is that, in an era of cultural revolution, considerable energy is expended in—and conflicts perpetuated by—protecting values and social systems that already are obsolete or nonfunctional. An alternative response to change is to accept it as a reality and to learn to anticipate and manage it. The paradox inherent in the problem of change is that the forces that contribute to resistance to change (e.g., values, beliefs, social institutions) are the same as those that ensure personal and social stability. The second response, thus, requires that people learn to adjust to the *process* of change rather than seek or invest themselves in values or norms that are static in nature.

Intra- or interpersonal change also may be threatening or rewarding. Such changes can threaten the basic concepts that people have of themselves, the strategies or devices that they use to maintain personal comfort and security, and the existence of interpersonal relations that are highly significant to them. On the other hand, individuals grow through changes in the ways that they see themselves and their relationships with others and in the extent to which they can accept themselves and take more responsibility for their lives.

Resistance to Change

Resistance is an emotional response to any change in a status quo that is perceived (realistically or unrealistically) as more comfortable or secure than the unknown quality of something different. It can occur even when the change is perceived as a source of satisfaction and/or self-enhancement. Indeed, some changes may be perceived as so threatening that groups or individuals may engage in resistant behavior that appears to be unproductive at best and self-destructive at worst. In therapy, as well as in training groups, the goal (intellectually) may be some type of personal or professional growth, but the emotional road to that goal may be fraught with disturbances of the status quo in a variety of areas that trigger all kinds of resistance maneuvers. Because this resistance to change may be an automatic response, people and groups often need to be aided in comparing the possible consequences of avoiding the change with those of helping to guide it.

Programs that involve examination and discussion of attitudes, beliefs, feelings, communication patterns, leadership styles, decision-making procedures, and so on, also have to deal with problems of change. The persons designing such programs must incorporate strategies to deal with resistance so that learning can take place. Many conflicts generated by change require new approaches and orientations for their management or resolution. It is important to recognize that resistance is not an isolated phenomenon but has a background that may be embedded in family, group, or cultural norms that are violated by the change program. It is, therefore, important to accept the resistance and the feelings behind it as legitimate and to work with it from there. To meet resistance with antagonism or pressure to change will increase the resistance and may foster a counterdependent attitude.

Change always involves some conflict or stress. The ways in which the conflict or stress is managed or resolved can be critical to the effectiveness of any attempt to solve problems. Because this is true on any level, the participants in a training program must be taught to deal with such conflict or stress and also must see the pertinent techniques modeled within the ongoing processes of the training program. In this way, they can learn experientially that conflict itself is neither good nor bad; the way conflict is handled, however, can have positive or negative consequences.

One important way in which conflict is handled is through resistance. In human relations training, forms of participant resistance include:

1. Rebelling, attacking or ridiculing the trainers or other members, being abusive or unreachable, or refusing to participate in or comply with group or workshop activities. These resistances frequently occur when an individual is severely threatened or does not want to be in the workshop (e.g., was sent or coerced into attending).
2. Frequently being tardy or absent, appearing reluctant to participate, leaving the group early, going in and out during sessions, or showing up at the wrong place or at the wrong time.
3. Acting confused or unaware of what is going on, blocking, misunderstanding, not getting the point.
4. Jumping from topic to topic, repeatedly being off target, introducing irrelevant topics or discussions, staying in the abstract, keeping things general rather than specific, intellectualizing, beating about the bush, talking *about* rather

than *to* other people, not looking at person to whom one is talking, being excessively polite or indirect rather than straightforward and direct, using excessive jargon or stereotyped language, or staying in the past or future when the present is more relevant.

5. Appearing not to see things as important or not to take them seriously, laughing off what others say, kidding around or using humor excessively, belittling others, or keeping others from getting close or making contact.

6. Not being in touch with or owning one's feelings, being unaware of one's body and bodily sensations, experiencing no or mild emotions (as a substitute for strong feelings), frequently being tired or sleepy during sessions, not being able to sit still, having headaches, backaches, or dizziness, or frequent crying.

These negative ways of coping with personal and interpersonal experiences are common to most groups. Such behaviors are usually individual reactions that happen to arise in a group setting rather than group-centered themes.

If these behaviors emerge sporadically, in isolation, or involve few group members, the trainer may intervene spontaneously and choose to work with them directly. If an issue appears to be more widespread or becomes a group norm, the trainer may choose a structured intervention to highlight the issue. For example, if group members are dealing with deviant behavior in a destructive way, a structured activity on conformity/deviation in which members exchange roles may be appropriate. Common resistance behaviors, such as crying, may stem from more than one source. If the trainer can determine the reason for the behavior, it can be dealt with more effectively.

Crying

Crying is a way of handling an emotion, be it sadness, happiness, anger, pity, etc. When crying is an expression of self-pity or self-commiseration, the trainer may allow the person to continue crying and ask the person what he or she is feeling and experiencing at that time. When crying is the expression of a release of tension, the trainer can encourage the person to continue crying but *not* give physical support such as holding or cradling. When crying is an expression of sadness, remorse, or guilt, the trainer can give the person support by verbal or physical contact and encourage the person to continue to talk about the experience, that is, to continue to describe what is happening in terms of bodily sensations, feelings or emotions, and whatever attitudes or images arise. At this point, the person may be encouraged *not* to try to "figure out" anything but merely to note what is happening without evaluating or adding anything to the experience. If other group members are curious or uncomfortable, the trainer can explain what is happening. Once members see the effects of staying with an experience, they show less tendency to move in immediately on a distressed individual. Rather, they will create space for the distressed individual to experience whatever is happening and will give support for this new way of behaving.

Theorizing

Thinking (the noise in the back of one's head) can get in the way of experiencing. We try to rationalize or justify many of our experiences in terms of cause-and-effect relationships and/or some personal or "scientific" theories. The question of what is real frequently becomes lost when the theory seems "more real" than the actual experience. Participants may need to be reminded that theory is just a point of view and is not a substitute for experience. Experience itself is neither right nor wrong, good nor bad, fair nor unfair; it merely occurs. The trainer and the participants must strive to become as aware as possible of the other persons' reactions and moods as they are experienced, without evaluating or adding anything to them. This involves putting aside one's own point of view in order to be open to others. The resistance to putting aside one's own point of view temporarily derives from the risk that one may be influenced to change it.

Avoiding Experience

Participants frequently do not allow themselves or others to experience whatever is happening to them at the time, as in the example of people moving in to give support to a person who is having a negative experience. This reaction, however, can cut off the experience. The participants are acting out their own needs to have that person feel good or to protect themselves from negative feelings. In addition to cutting off the experience, overly supportive or consoling action by the group may indicate to the member in distress the group's feelings that he or she cannot "handle" the negative experience. If the trainer "cradles" the individual, it serves to take that particular participant out of the action and put him or her in "protective custody." This initial impulse to soothe others may need to be put aside if it will benefit the individuals (and the group) to work through the difficulty.

There are many ways in which people can avoid experiences, particularly those that they find uncomfortable. They can rationalize the discomfort, justify it, create a cause-and-effect relationship, smoke a cigarette, act it out physically in some way, cry, accuse or verbally attack others, and so on. The most frequent method used by group members to avoid experience is to "tell their stories"— that is, to go into lengthy, detailed discussions of what happened to whom and to offer theories as to why the individuals behaved as they did. This tactic takes the individual *away* from the experience, since describing it puts one in the role of observer. If the story is repeated, the teller becomes even more removed from the experience and the feelings behind the original experience no longer are active. The trainer must be alert to this type of resistance to experiencing the here and now and may need to encourage participants to support the group's norm to remain in the present and stay with the experience.

Rebellion[1]

There are two points in a training workshop when strong resistance or open rebellion are most likely to occur. The first is in the beginning of a workshop and occurs among participants who have been "drafted" or sent or who have some negative prejudices about the upcoming experience. The workshop design can address itself to this resistance without becoming an apology for experiential learning. As has been stated, resistance usually is an expression of here-and-now feelings, and should be acknowledged. In many

---

[1]This discussion of rebellion was adapted from materials written by Joyce Paris for the TIGER handbook.

instances, resistance expresses a pessimism about human affairs that is difficult to maintain in a setting that is supportive.

The classic point for rebellion to emerge is about three-fourths of the way through a workshop. The participants may be expressing some intuitive group-level need if they choose the three-quarter point to rebel, because enough time has passed to justify their position yet sufficient time remains for reconciliation and mutual success. It is wise to determine whether or not the resistance reflects general community feeling. Sometimes this assessment in itself is sufficient and the community will decide to continue, perhaps because the right to resist has been recognized. However, if the resistance is more widespread, the only appropriate response is to put the workshop design aside and listen to the participants' needs.

One of the paradoxes of the experiential learning method is that although it includes such norms and values as participatory decision making, open expression of feelings, and democratic involvement, the trainer often behaves like a circus trainer, cracking the whip of instruction, calling time, and generally ordering people around. (This style is described by Charles Seashore as "Permissive Fascism.") Generally, the more structured and complex the design, the more this is true. In addition, the trainer is not equally vulnerable with the participants. Therefore, it often is wise to suspend the design and allow the participants to influence the workshop or modify the next module of time. Although the resultant design may resemble a "free university," the process of shifting responsibility to the participants (so that the design is a joint product of staff and participants) usually is productive, and fresh cooperation usually emerges.

Assuming Responsibility for Change

Most people think of change as some kind of action one takes to produce new behaviors and attitudes consistent with a desired goal or mode. In one sense, changing oneself to be something other than what one is would result in an inauthentic person. One point of view is that human beings already are perfect but, in the process of growing up, have been trained to cover up this perfection. The process of change, then, would not imply changing into something else, but discovering who one really is. Such change occurs when a person assumes complete responsibility for his or her experience or for what is real for that person. That is, one creates whatever experience one has had in the past, is having in the present, and will have in the future. Since all experience originates from the individual, only the individual can change his or her own experience. Although all persons are affected by external events over which they have no control, it is in their power to change how they perceive and deal with those events. People cannot change other people; they can change themselves in ways that may affect how other people relate to them. Accepting responsibility for personal change involves three steps:

Awareness

Most people live in a state of unawareness, occasionally awakening to experience what is happening around them. Awareness means being attuned not only to what is going on with oneself but also involves being attuned to what is going on with others and actively attending to (listening and seeing) them. Being aware means paying attention to what is happening in the here and now rather than attending to the noise (thinking) in the back of one's mind. It is difficult to be aware of the *now* when one's attention is focused either on the past or the future.

When a person is unaware, much information (feelings, beliefs, attitudes) lies below the level of the person's consciousness and is not available to be used in making choices and decisions. As a consequence, the person does not take charge of his or her own life by making choices more deliberately. Awareness is the vehicle for conducting one's life in a more *intentional* way. At times, being aware involves merely a willingness just to *be* with oneself or another person and just to experience what is happening. Increased awareness frequently results in assuming responsibility for creating one's own experience and enhances the ability to choose what that experience is going to be like.

Acceptance

Acceptance means accepting what *is* without evaluating or judging how it should be and whether or not it is right or wrong, good or bad, or trying to justify, rationalize, or make sense out of whatever is happening. What *is* happening to each person is what is *true* for that person. If a person can accept a behavior without evaluating it or justifying it in terms of some historical antecedents, then he or she can change that behavior. One cannot change one's own behavior without owning and accepting it. Similarly, if one can accept another person's behavior without evaluating it, one can help to create a climate in which that other person will feel freer to choose to change or not to change.

Lack of acceptance generally is the root of most personal and interpersonal problems. Most people have models of how they and other people should or should not behave. These models are based on expectations. Usually, if these expectations are violated, people throw away the other person (terminate the relationship) and keep the model. Very seldom are the models or expectations examined or discarded. A person who has less stringent expectations, who is more accepting, is generally less frustrated, less upset, and more successful in interpersonal relationships.

In terms of group issues, members will frequently become upset because they are not feeling the way that they think other group members are feeling. For example, some members might say that they are upset because they do not feel closer to certain other group members. They *think* that they should feel closer. The trainer can ask these members if they can accept the fact they do not feel closer without evaluating their feelings as being good or bad, right or wrong, i.e., whether they can stop "hassling" themselves about not feeling the way they think they should feel. If members can (a) accept whatever experience they are having as real for them at that moment, (b) note what is happening, (c) resist the urge to evaluate the experience, and (d) share what is happening to them with other group members, they can then move on.

Sharing

One kind of sharing involves using other people as sounding boards to obtain reactions and feedback regarding their feelings and perceptions about what one says or does. Another kind of sharing is to have other people listen to what one is trying to communicate. The purpose of this type of sharing is not to have others agree or disagree, evaluate what is being said, or give their reactions; it is merely to share one's awareness with someone else. Sharing in this sense is not telling one's life "story" or relating past history but relating what one is currently experiencing.

Both types of sharing can be used effectively in the workshop setting to help participants learn to focus on the here and now and to help them to become aware that exploring an experience tends to "complete" it. Participants can be asked to think about inter-actions they currently are involved in that are frustrating or upsetting. These interactions usually involve some feelings, expec-tations, or thoughts that people do not share with others. The trainer can point out the fact that because these experiences are not shared, people usually become obsessed with what they should have done or said and work out the interactions to satisfactory conclusions in their fantasies in order to be "finished" with them.

One consequence of avoiding completion of an experience is that the experience or feeling persists in spite of the individual's best efforts. What usually happens is that the feelings go "under-ground" and later are acted out in indirect ways. It is a paradox that when people attempt to control their feelings by suppressing or denying them, they actually lose control of them. For example, one group member may become irritated repeatedly about the way another group member is behaving. The first member can tell herself continually that she should not feel that way and can engage in self-analysis of why she feels as she does. By imposing a standard on herself about how she should or should not feel, she resists the experience and refuses to accept it. If the trainer tells this person that it is acceptable to have such feelings and validates their reality, the member will then feel relief and can be encouraged to allow herself to experience and share her feelings without attempting to rationalize or justify them. Frequently, during this process, the person will discover that the feelings have dissipated or that she has become aware of what really was bothering her.

Completion

When group members are allowed to complete the experience they are having, there is a sense of "having done with it." Completing the experience creates space for members to move on and diminishes the possibility that events in the past will affect their behavior in the future. Completion of the experience leaves no clutter; participants can become more clear about their intentions and are better able to communicate. The willingness to share not only aids completion but also facilitates a greater acceptance of what is true or real for a person, and, as a consequence of greater acceptance, the potential for change is greater.

Change, then, is a here-and-now phenomenon; it cannot occur either in the past or in the future. Change does not have to be a conscious effort to modify some behavior. It may be a by-product of a greater awareness of one's own experience, a willingness to accept that experience as real without evaluating it, a willingness to share that experience, and a willingness to experience such sharing in the here and now. A completed experience leaves no unfinished business; it provides the space to change or to create a new experience. The key to change, therefore, is to remain in the *present*, to *experience* what is happening, and to *choose* what one will do or not do.

REFERENCES

Blake, R.R., Mouton, J.S., & Blansfield, M.C. *Team action laboratory*. Dallas, TX: Internal Revenue Service, 1961.

Bovard, E.W., Jr. Group structure and perception. In D. Cartwright & A. Zander (Eds.), *Group dynamics*. New York: Harper & Row, 1953.

Lewin, K. Frontiers in group dynamics: I. Concept, method, and reality in social sciences: Social equilibria and social change. *Human Relations*, 1947, *1*(1), 5-41.

Schein, E.H. Management development, human relations training, and the process of influence. In I.R. Wechsler & E.H. Schein (Eds.), *Issues in training*. Arlington, VA: National Training Laboratories (Selected Reading Series 5), 1962, 47-60.

Wechsler, I.R., Massarik, F., & Tannenbaum, R. The self in process: A sensitivity training emphasis. In I.R. Wechsler & E.H. Schein (Eds.), *Issues in training*. Arlington, VA: National Training Laboratories (Selected Reading Series 5), 1962, 33-46.

Chapter 3
Feedback in Training Groups

FEEDBACK AS A STEERING APPARATUS[1]

The process of giving, asking for, and receiving feedback is probably the most important dimension in human relations training. Indeed, the exchange of feedback is a crucial communication process in any interpersonal relationship. It is through feedback that we can learn "to see ourselves as others see us." Giving or "sending" feedback is a verbal or nonverbal process through which an individual lets others know his or her perceptions and feelings about *their* behavior. When *soliciting* feedback, an individual is asking for others' perceptions and feelings about his or her own behavior.

Feedback as a means of exchanging personal impressions and reactions is seldom used intentionally in everyday social interactions and, when used, is seldom effective in providing a learning experience for the recipient. In the training environment, however, feedback can be exchanged in relative safety; it is the primary method by which participants develop more effective ways to monitor and assess the impact of their ongoing interactions. In an atmosphere in which choice of one's behavior and ownership of that behavior are stressed, participants can use feedback to help them make choices about changing or not changing their behavior and to test whether or not attempted changes actually are achieved.

_____

[1]Adapted from Philip G. Hanson, "Giving Feedback: An Interpersonal Skill," in John E. Jones & J. William Pfeiffer (Eds.), *The 1975 Annual Handbook for Group Facilitators*, San Diego, CA: University Associates, 1975.

The term "feedback" was borrowed from rocket engineering by Kurt Lewin (1947, 1951), a founder of laboratory education. A rocket sent into space contains a mechanism that sends signals back to Earth. A steering apparatus on Earth receives these signals, makes adjustments if the rocket is off target, and corrects the course. Within the training group, members can perform the function of the steering apparatus for each other by sending signals to members who are off target in terms of the learning goals they have set for themselves.

It is not easy to give feedback so that it can be accepted without threat by another individual. To master the technique, one must have courage, sensitivity to other people's needs, and the ability to put oneself in another's shoes. In the human relations training workshop, emphasis is placed on developing attitudes of caring, trust, acceptance, openness, and concern for the needs of others. For most participants, the hardest learning is the ability to let other people be as they are, not as the participants would like them to be. The willingness to accept things as they are in the here and now is a primary prerequisite for giving and receiving feedback effectively and for using that feedback for one's own growth.

Norms for giving and asking for feedback must be continuously supported by the training staff, even when the feedback takes place spontaneously in the group (Luft, 1970). Systematic feedback sessions, complemented by the use of instruments, can help to ensure that each member participates and receives some information regarding his or her behavior from everyone in the group. Structured feedback also can be introduced by having members fill out scales describing their reactions to the group in terms of group structure, atmosphere, and cohesion, and in terms of the degree of openness or level of participation of each member.

THE INFORMATION-EXCHANGE PROCESS

Between two people, the process of feedback exchange is as follows (Figure 1): person A's *intention* is to act in relation to person B, who sees only person A's *behavior*. Between the intention and the behavior is an encoding process that person A uses to ensure that his intentions and behavior are congruent. Person B perceives person A's behavior, decodes it (an interpreting process), and intends to respond. Between person B's intention and responding behavior there is also an encoding process. Person A then perceives person B's responding behavior and decodes it.

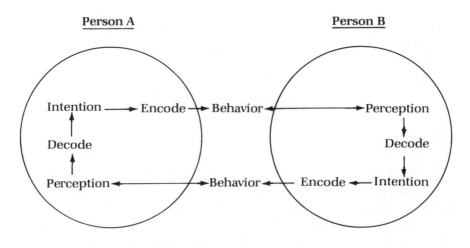

Figure 1. Giving and Receiving Feedback: A Circular Communication Process

If either person's encoding or decoding process is ineffective, the receiver may respond in a manner that will confuse the sender. For example, if one group member's intention is to compliment another by saying, "I really admire Joan's leadership of this group," the first member may be surprised if Joan responds by saying, "I am not leading the group; if I don't talk, no one else will!" Joan's decoding process leads her to hear the message as implying that she was dominating the group. The problem here is that a number of things may have contributed to Joan's response: (a) she may have misread the intention (decoding problem), (b) the sender's statement (behavior) may not have been congruent with his intention (encoding problem), or (c) Joan may actually have read the intention behind the statement correctly, that is, the sender's intention may have been to "put her down" in the guise of a compliment.

Thus, the practice of giving and receiving feedback can help people to discover whether or not their behavior is congruent with their intentions because the process focuses on *behavior* (only they know their intentions). Furthermore, the process highlights the fact that people frequently tend to give feedback about *other* people's intentions, rather than their behavior. By practicing and perfecting one's skill in giving and receiving feedback, one can learn more and more to stay within the here-and-now reality of a situation (the behavior) and can learn to manage the impulse to focus attention on unobservable matters (speculations about intentions, reasons, etc.).

Responsibility for Feedback

The question that frequently arises during feedback exchanges is: how much responsibility should the sender assume for his behavior and the receiver for her response? This question is especially pertinent if the feedback is negative or if it evokes a negative or defensive response. Some people are willing to assume more than their share of responsibility for anything and other people may refuse to accept any responsibility—even for their own behavior. It is the function of the trainer to guide the group members in exploring their reactions to and utilization of the feedback process. For example, if George is habitually late for the group meetings, he may receive feedback from other members concerning their reactions to his behavior. His response may be to point out to the group members their lack of tolerance for individual differences. He may say that the group members are attempting to limit his freedom and that they seem to be investing too much responsibility in him for the group's effectiveness; he wants to be involved in the group, but does not understand why he needs to be on time.

This situation presents a value dilemma to the group: freedom of choice to change versus pressure to conform. George's observations are accurate, but his behavior is provocative. One way of clarifying this dilemma is to point out that although George is responsible only for his own behavior, the reactions of others inevitably affect him. To the extent that he cares about the others in the group or his relationship with them, he must consider their responses as information to be used in choosing what his interactions with them will be like.

GUIDELINES FOR GIVING FEEDBACK

It is possible to minimize people's defensiveness about receiving feedback and to maximize their ability to use it for their own personal growth. Feedback must be given in such a way that the person receiving it can *hear* it in the most objective and least distorted way possible, *understand* it, and *choose* to *use* it or *not* to use it. Regardless of how accurate the feedback may be, if individuals cannot accept the information because they are too defensive, the feedback is useless.

The guidelines that follow are listed as if they were bipolar, with the first term in each dimension describing the more effective method of giving feedback.

Direct/Indirect Expression of Feelings

Joe, intending to compliment Marie, says to her, "I wish I could be more selfish, like you." Marie responds, "Why you insensitive boor, what do you mean by saying I'm selfish?" Joe then becomes defensive and retaliates, and the situation rapidly degenerates. Part of the problem here is that Marie hid her hurt feelings behind name-calling. Instead, Marie could have given Joe feedback by stating her feelings directly; that is, she could have said, "When you said you wished you could be more selfish, like me, I felt angry and put down." This method of giving feedback contains positive elements that the first does not. In her initial response, Marie stated her feelings *indirectly;* if she had described them *directly* ("I felt angry and put down"), Joe could have seen clearly what her feelings were and what specific behavior of his ("when you said you wished you could be more selfish like me") triggered these feelings. He might then feel more free to respond positively to her.

If Tom says to Andy, "I like you," he is expressing his feelings directly, risking rejection. However, if he says, "You are a likeable person," the risk is less. Indirect expression of feelings is safer because it is ambiguous and offers an escape from commitment. (If confronted, Tom could deny his own feelings because he has not expressed them directly.) However, it frequently gives only half the message, and the receiver may easily misinterpret the giver's intent.

"You are driving too fast" is an indirect expression of feelings. "I am anxious because you are driving so fast" is a direct expression of feelings. It is obvious that, in the second case, the giver retains responsibility for his or her own feelings rather than attempting to coerce the receiver into assuming the responsibility. It is thus easier for the receiver to hear the message without becoming defensive and cutting off the possibility of acting on the message.

Indirect statements often begin with "I feel that . . . " and finish with a perception, belief, or opinion; for example, "I feel that you are angry." The clue that this type of statement really means "think" and not "feel" is the use of the word "that." "I feel that . . . " almost always means "This is what I really think." "I feel anxious because you look angry" expresses the speaker's feelings directly and also states a perception. The use of the word "feel" is usually authentic when it is followed by a "feeling" (sad, happy, irritated, relieved, etc.). In the workshop setting, participants may need to practice giving and receiving *feeling* messages before they can understand this distinction fully.

Description/Interpretation of Behavior

When Marie says to Joe, "When you said you wished you could be more selfish, like me, I felt angry and put down," Marie is *describing the behavior* to which she is reacting. She is not *attributing a motive* to Joe's behavior, e.g., "You are hostile" or "You do not like me." When one attributes a motive to another person's behavior, one is interpreting that person's *intention*. Since his intention is private and known only to him, any interpretation of his behavior is highly questionable.

In addition, the first person's interpretation may arise from a theory of personality that is not shared by the second person. For example, if William is fidgeting in his chair and shuffling his feet and Walter says, "You are anxious," Walter is interpreting William's behavior. Walter's theory of personality states that when a person fidgets in his chair and shuffles his feet, he is manifesting anxiety. Such a theory interposed between two people can create a barrier between them that precludes understanding. The effectiveness of this barrier can be increased if the receiver's theory conflicts with the giver's. If, instead, Walter *describes* William's behavior, William may then explain his behavior by saying, "My foot is falling asleep."

In any event, interpreting other people's behavior or ascribing motives to it tends to put them on the defensive and cause them to spend their energies on either explaining the behavior or defending themselves. It deprives them of the opportunity to interpret or make sense of their own behavior and may create dependency on the interpreter, particularly if the interpreter is seen as powerful. Such feedback, regardless of how much insight it actually contains, can rarely be used positively.

Nonevaluative/Evaluative Feedback

When giving feedback, one must respond not to the personal worth of the receiver, but to the person's *behavior*. An individual who is told that he is "stupid" or "insensitive" will have great difficulty in responding objectively. A person may sometimes *act* stupidly or *behave* in an insensitive way, but that does not mean that the person is, by nature, stupid or insensitive. In addition to assuming the role of judge, the giver of evaluative feedback assumes that he or she can distinguish categorically between "good" and "bad" or between "right" and "wrong." Such a person may even be surprised when the receiver does not accept the feedback because of the values on which it is based.

It is difficult for people to respond to evaluative feedback because it usually offends their feelings of self-worth or self-esteem. These are core concepts about ourselves that cannot be changed readily by feedback, nor can they be interpreted easily in terms of actual behavior. It is difficult to point out to an individual the specific *behaviors* that manifest many evaluative concepts. If, for example, Joe were to be given feedback that he is "stupid," he probably would not know what *behaviors* he was expected to change. In addition, evaluative feedback frequently engenders defensiveness. When this occurs, the feedback is not likely to be useful or even heard. One way to avoid this is to frame the feedback in terms of the *effect* of the receiver's behavior *on* the sender.

Specific/General Feedback

By describing a *specific* behavior, the giver of feedback tells the receiver to which behavior the giver is reacting. General terms such as "hostile" or "anxious" or "stupid" do not specify *what* evoked the feedback response. Again, the receiver would not know what behavior to change. Even positive feedback expressed in general terms, such as "You are a warm person," does not allow the receiver to know what specific behavior is perceived as warm and, thus, the receiver cannot expand or build on the desired behavior. Again, the complete statement would be something like "When you defended Tom, I felt relieved and grateful to you."

Freedom of Choice/Pressure to Change

If feedback is understood by and important to the receiver, he will probably act on it. If it is not important to him, he may choose not to utilize it. Sometimes an expectation develops in groups that if a member is given feedback he or she *should* act on it, e.g., change the behavior in question. The sequence of feedback and change is not automatic. People should have the freedom to use feedback in any way that is meaningful to them. Imposing standards or demands for change on other people and expecting them to conform arouses resistance and resentment. Such pressures, whether direct or subtle, usually create a win-lose relationship.

Expression of Disappointment as Feedback

Sometimes feedback reflects the sender's disappointment that the receiver did not meet the sender's expectations or hopes. For example, a group leader may be disappointed that some members did not live up to their potential impact on the group or a professor may be disappointed in a student's lack of achievement. These situations represent a dilemma. An important part of the sender's expression of feedback is his or her own feelings, including disappointment or satisfaction. If the sender withholds these feelings, the receiver may be given a false impression. If, however, the sender expresses the disappointment, the receiver may experience the feedback as an indication of personal failure instead of an incentive to change. The sender can resolve part of the dilemma by stating that the feelings and expectations are the sender's *own,* stemming from his or her *own needs,* and that it is not the *responsibility* of the *receiver* to satisfy these feelings or expectations. If the feedback reflects a caring attitude, the receiver may choose to perceive it as encouragement to change.

Persistent Behavior

Frequently the complaint is heard that some group members persist in behaviors that others find irritating, despite the feedback they receive to that effect. The most the members can do in this case is to continue to confront the offenders with their feelings. In the case of George, for example, although he clearly has the freedom not to change, he also may have to accept the consequences of his decision, i.e., other members' continued irritation about his absences and the likelihood of their punitive reactions. One cannot reasonably expect other group members to feel positive toward one and also to accept a behavior that they find irritating.

Reinforcement of Change

If a member changes a behavior and then does not receive positive feedback regarding the new behavior, the change may not become permanent. However, it is possible that the change may bring about positive or reinforcing consequences other than verbal feedback. For example, as a by-product of change in an individual, other people may change their behavior in relation to that individual. These new responses gradually will become more appropriate to the changed behavior on the part of the first individual.

Immediate/Delayed Timing

To be most effective, feedback should be given immediately after the behavior that prompts it. If time elapses, the receiver may not remember saying or doing the thing in question and other group members may not remember the event. Its significance to other group members may be much less than its significance to the giver of the feedback. When feedback is given immediately after the behavior in question, it acts as a mirror of that behavior, reflecting back to the doer. Also, the event is fresh in everyone's mind and other group members can contribute their observations about the feedback interaction.

The tendency to delay feedback arises from people's fears of losing control of their feelings, hurting other people's feelings, or exposing themselves to other people's criticism. Nevertheless, although the here-and-now transactions of group life often can be the most threatening, they also can be the most exciting and growth producing.

Planned Feedback

An exception to the norm of giving immediate feedback is the periodic feedback session, which is planned to keep communication channels open. In these sessions, participants cover events that occurred since the last session or work with material generated during the current meeting. For this process to be effective, however, the decision to have these feedback sessions or to establish a goal for spontaneous feedback should be reached through consensus of the participants.

Group-Shared/External Feedback

When feedback is given immediately after the event, it usually is group shared, so that other members can observe the interaction as it occurs and, perhaps, comment on the appropriateness of its elements. If group members support the sender's feelings and perceptions (consensual validation), the feedback has more potency. If the sender's feedback is not supported by the group members, then the sender would have to look at his or her own behavior and its appropriateness.

Events that occur outside the group (there and then) may be known to only one or two group members and, consequently, cannot be reacted to or discussed meaningfully by other participants, who may feel left out. Because perceptions of outside events are colored by the teller's own biases, these events are not valid material for the other group members to give feedback on. Members may listen empathically to the speakers or ask questions for clarification about the events; but commenting on there-and-then (out of the group) interactions is not the same as giving feedback on events that have occurred in the group.

Use of There-and-Then Material

The relation of there-and-then events to the here and now, and vice versa, can be productive when used as a bridge between the two. It also can be productive if some members have had long-term relationships with one another. It is important, however, to recognize both the necessity and the difficulty of involving other group members in such discussions in meaningful ways.

Consistent Perceptions

Part of each group member's responsibility is to ask for feedback from members who are not responding so the receiver will know how everyone sees his or her behavior. Group members may tend to agree or disagree privately when someone else is giving feedback. The receiver may have to be somewhat aggressive and persistent in seeking this information. Feedback from only one person may present a distorted picture because that person's perceptions of the event may differ from those of the other group members. When all members' reactions are given, however, the receiver has a more representative view of his or her behavior from a much broader perspective. If the group members are consistent in their perception of the receiver's behavior, and this disagrees with the receiver's self-perception, then the receiver needs to look more closely at the validity of the self-perception. Even if group members are not in agreement, the fact that people perceive an individual's behavior differently is useful information in itself. When *all* the data have been collected, the receiver is in a better position to make a decision about how to use the feedback.

Solicited/Imposed Feedback

In most exchanges, feedback is imposed. People give feedback whether or not it is solicited and whether or not the other person is prepared to receive it. In addition, the sender's need to give feedback may be much greater than the receiver's need to receive it. This is particularly true when the sender is upset about something concerning the potential recipient. In many situations it is legitimate to impose feedback, particularly when a norm exists for giving as well as for soliciting feedback or in order to induce a norm of spontaneity. However, feedback usually is more helpful when a person solicits it. By asking for feedback, the receiver indicates a willingness to listen and a desire to know how others perceive his or her behavior.

In asking for feedback, it is important to follow some of the same guidelines as in giving feedback. For example, people should be specific about the subjects on which they want feedback. Individuals who say to the group, "I would like the group to tell me what they think about me" may receive more feedback than they planned. In addition, the request is so general that the group members may be uncertain about where to begin or which behaviors are relevant to the request. In these cases, other group members can help the receiver by asking questions such as "Can you be more specific?" or "About what do you want feedback?" Feedback is a reciprocal process; both senders and receivers can help each other in soliciting and in giving it.

Sometimes it is also important to provide feedback on *how* a person is *giving* feedback. If a receiver is upset, hurt, or angry, other group members can say to the sender, "I, too, feel angry about what you just said to Tom" or "What other way could you have given the relevant information without evaluating or degrading Tom?"

Many people want to know how their behavior is perceived by others but fear the consequences of asking for such information. How easily people will ask for feedback is related to the trust they have in their relationships. One unfortunate consequence of giving feedback is that the receivers may misuse it to reinforce their negative feelings about themselves. This is particularly true of people who have negative self-images. When individuals appear to be using feedback to "put themselves down" or to confirm questionable feelings about their self-esteem, it is helpful to point out what is happening. If this is not done and the process continues, other members eventually may stop giving feedback to the individuals in question because they may begin to feel guilty about "loading it on" those individuals.

Focus on Easy-to-Control/Difficult-to-Control Behavior

To be effective, feedback should be aimed at behavior that is relatively easy to change. Many individuals' behaviors, however, are habitual and are developed through years of behaving and responding in certain ways. Feedback on these kinds of behaviors is often frustrating because the behaviors may be very difficult to change. Repeated negative feedback about such a behavior (e.g., smoking, biting one's nails) can lead to a sense of failure if the receiver has been unable to change the behavior. In fact, behaviors that serve to reduce tension may be increased as tension builds in the individual as a result of pressure to change.

In giving feedback, one frequently must determine whether or not the behavior in question represents a mere habit or is the result of a deep emotional or other factor. Sometimes it may be helpful to ask whether or not the receiver perceives the behavior to be modifiable. Many behaviors, however, can be changed relatively easily through feedback and the individual's conscious desire to change.

Motivation to Help[2]/Motivation to Hurt

It is assumed that the primary motivation for participation in human relations training is to help oneself and, at the same time, to facilitate the growth of others. When individuals are angry, however, their motives may change to hurting the people toward whom the anger is directed. Frequently, the conflict turns into a win-lose confrontation in which the goal of the interaction is to degrade the other person. It is difficult when one is angry to consider that the needs of the other person are as important as one's own. Feedback that is motivated by anger generally is useless, even when the information is potentially helpful, because the receiver may need to reject the feedback in order to protect his own self-image.

Coping with Anger

There are several ways to cope with anger. One is to engage in a verbal or physical attack; another method is to suppress it. One consequence of suppression, however, is that internal pressure builds to the point where one may lose control of one's behavior

---

[2]The word "help" as used here means "to help the relationship to be more productive and satisfying." It is not used in the sense of the helper-helpee relationship.

and act out the feelings destructively. A third, and better, method is to acknowledge and talk about personal feelings of anger without assigning responsibility for them to another person. In this way the anger dissipates without being acted on or suppressed. Anger and conflict are not in themselves "bad"; they are as legitimate as any other feelings. In fact, conflict can be growth producing. It is the manner in which conflict or angry feelings are handled that can have negative consequences. Only through surfacing and resolving conflicts can people develop competence and confidence in dealing with them. Part of the benefit derived from human relations training groups is learning to express anger or to resolve conflicts in constructive, problem-solving ways.

Applying These Guidelines

The process of giving feedback obviously would be hampered if one simultaneously attempted to consider *all* the guidelines given in this chapter. Some are needed more frequently than others, e.g., feedback should be descriptive, nonevaluative, and specific, and should embody freedom of choice; one learns to apply these guidelines through practice.

The preceding guidelines also can be used diagnostically. For example, if the person receiving feedback reacts defensively, some of the guidelines probably have been violated. Group members can ask how the receiver heard the feedback and can help the giver to assess how it was given.

GUIDELINES FOR RECEIVING FEEDBACK

The responsibility for the potential usefulness of feedback lies not only with the giver but also with the receiver. Even though the giver may have utilized all the preceding guidelines, the receiver may still reject, distort, or misunderstand the feedback. There are many people who are not ready or able (for whatever reason) to hear any "criticism" of their behavior without negatively judging themselves or the giver in a way that discourages any further exchange of this kind of information. The problem for the trainer and other group members is to be sensitive to these issues and, at the same time, to not be manipulated or coerced into supporting the norm of playing it safe or avoiding confrontation. Group members who are extremely anxious about the feedback process can exert considerable pressure, directly or indirectly, on other group members to avoid or dilute their exchanges. A resolution of this issue is to create norms for the exchange of honest feedback and, at the same time, to reinforce norms of encouragement and support rather than for pressure, conformity, or reciprocity. The norms can be facilitated by spelling out ways of receiving feedback that will minimize the tendency to defend against it.

Understanding What Was Said

On receiving feedback, the receiver should make certain that he understands it and should test out his understanding of it with the giver. This may include asking for clarification and amplification and repeating what he heard so that the giver can verify his perception or provide further clarification. The feedback also can be checked with other group members to see if they have the same or different perceptions.

Being Open Rather than Defensive

The recipient of feedback should try to avoid *explaining* the behavior, giving *reasons* or *causes* for it, or immediately rejecting the feedback as invalid. Since the feedback represents another person's experience or reality, it is neither right nor wrong. Immediately rejecting feedback or defending against it shuts off the possibility of adequately understanding other people's perceptions and of examining these perceptions in relation to one's own behavior.

Checking the "Fit"

After checking for understanding and soliciting more than one person's perception, the receiver of feedback should compare the actual behavior in question with the feedback about it. If the feedback "fits," the receiver can decide whether or not to attempt to change the behavior. If the feedback does not fit, it may be rejected or the receiver can decide to keep his options open. The second alternative, of course, is more productive for learning. Once one is alerted to the behaviors referred to in the feedback, one can watch to see if they occur in the future and may even solicit the aid of other members of the group to monitor the behavior in question.

Separating Oneself and One's Behavior

The receiver's attitude is critical to how or whether feedback will be used. If, for example, one experiences the feedback as a threat to one's sense of personal worth or adequacy, the potential benefit of the information may be lost. If the feedback confirms an already negative self-image, it may be misinterpreted or distorted beyond what was actually said. If, on the other hand, one is able to keep one's sense of personal value separate from the behaviors about which one is receiving feedback, the information obtained can have great potential for personal growth. The difference between the *person* and that person's *behavior* may have to be emphasized repeatedly.

THE PURPOSES OF FEEDBACK

Each of us has created our own reality concerning others and the world around us. We also participate in another reality "out there" that is reached through agreement. What we see in another individual is a consequence both of what we create and of what we can agree on. Feedback can help to make us more aware of ourselves by showing us how we are experienced from another individual's unique point of view and from the group's point of view. One person's experience of another is important in order to clarify the relationship between them, even if one's experience of the other is quite different from the group's experience of that person. One provides a unique experience, the other a social reality. Giving and receiving feedback, therefore, may serve several purposes:

1. Feedback from others helps us to be aware of their experience of us. It is a way of monitoring or checking how the relationship is going in the eyes of the other person or group.

2. Feedback enables us to know how we are progressing toward our goals. It can act as a corrective steering device when we deviate from the path toward our goals and can guide subsequent behavior in the desired direction.
3. Feedback enables us to know the effect of our behavior on others. It validates or invalidates our intentions in terms of what we actually do or say. That is, feedback serves as a check on reality.
4. Feedback enables us to compare our self-perceptions with the perceptions of others and help us to see ourselves as others do.
5. The process of giving and receiving feedback teaches us to be more observant about our own and others' behaviors and to distinguish, more accurately, what we observe from what we attribute.
6. As the norm for exchanging feedback develops in the group, a standard of objectivity also is established. Feedback about behavior is seen as information to be examined as any other kind of information would be.

A MODEL FOR SOLICITING AND GIVING FEEDBACK: THE JOHARI WINDOW[3]

The process of giving and receiving feedback can be illustrated by means of a model called the JoHari Window (Luft, 1969, 1970).[4] The model was developed by Joseph Luft, a psychologist, and Harry Ingram, a psychiatrist, for their program in group process. The model depicts a window through which communication flows as one gives and receives information about oneself and others.

---

[3]Adapted from Philip G. Hanson, "The JoHari Window: A Model for Soliciting and Giving Feedback," in John E. Jones & J. William Pfeiffer (Eds.), *The 1973 Annual Handbook for Group Facilitators*, San Diego, CA: University Associates, 1973.

[4]Luft's book, *Group Processes*, was originally published in 1963; 1970 is the date of the most current edition.

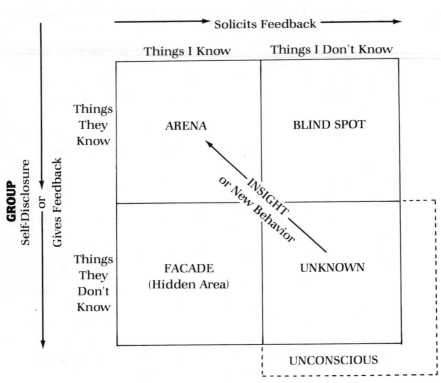

Figure 2. The JoHari Window

Four Types of Information About the Self

Looking at the four panes of the JoHari Window (Figure 2) in terms of columns (vertical) and rows (horizontal), the two columns represent the *self* and the two rows represent the *group.* Column one contains "things that I know about myself"; column two contains "things that I do not know about myself." Row one contains "things that the group knows about me"; row two contains "things that the group does not know about me." The information contained in these rows and columns is not static but moves from one pane to another as the level of mutual trust and the exchange of feedback varies in the group. As a consequence of this movement, the size and shape of the panes within the window vary.

The first pane, the *Arena*, contains things that I know about myself and about which the group knows. It is an area characterized by free and open exchange of information between myself and others. The behavior here is public and available to everyone. The Arena increases in size as the level of trust increases between individuals or between the individual and the group and as more information—particularly personally relevant information—is shared.

The second pane, the *Blind Spot*, contains information that I do *not* know about myself but of which the group may know. As I participate within the group, I communicate all kinds of information of which I am not aware, but which is picked up by other people. This information may be in the form of the things I say, the way in which I say things, mannerisms, or the style in which I relate to others. Knowledge of the extent to which we are insensitive to much of our own behavior and what it can communicate to others can be quite surprising and disconcerting. For example, a group member once told me that whenever I was asked to comment on a personal or group issue, I coughed before I answered.

In the third windowpane are the things that I know about myself but of which the group is unaware. For one reason or another, I keep this information hidden. For example, my fear may be that if the group members knew of my feelings, perceptions, or opinions about the group or individuals within the group, they might reject, attack, or hurt me in some way. As a consequence, I withhold this information. This pane is called the *Facade* or *Hidden Area*. One of the reasons why I may keep this information to myself is that I do not see supportive elements in the group; thus, my assumption is that if I reveal my feelings, thoughts, and reactions, the members of the group might judge me negatively. I cannot find out, however, how members will actually react to me unless I test my assumptions (take some risks) and reveal something of myself. On the other hand, I may keep certain kinds of information to myself when my motives for doing so are to control or manipulate others or when the information is not relevant to the group.

The last pane, the *Unknown*, contains things that neither I nor the group know about me. Some of this material may be so far below my level of consciousness that I may never become aware of it. Other material, however, may be below the surface of awareness of both myself and the group but can be made public through an exchange of feedback. This area represents such things as intrapersonal dynamics, early childhood memories, latent potential, and unrecognized resources.

Because one's internal boundaries can move backward and forward or up and down as a consequence of soliciting or giving feedback, it would be possible to have a window in which there would be no Unknown. However, knowing *all* about oneself is extremely unlikely; so the Unknown in the model is extended (the dotted line) so that part of it will always remain unknown. This extension might be compared to the Freudian "Unconscious."

Changing the Availability of Information About the Self

One goal that members may set for themselves in the group is to decrease their Blind Spots, i.e., move the vertical line to the right. Because this area contains information that the group members know about a member but of which that person is unaware, the only way the member can increase his or her awareness of this material is to obtain feedback from the group. As a consequence, each person must develop a receptive attitude and actively solicit feedback from the other group members in such a way that they will feel comfortable in giving it. The more one does this, the more one's vertical line will move to the right (Figure 3).

Another goal that members may set for themselves is to reduce their Facades, i.e., to move the horizontal line down. Because this area contains information that members have been keeping from the group, they can reduce their Facades by giving feedback to group members or the total group about their reactions to what is going on in the group and inside themselves. In this instance, they will be disclosing themselves in terms of their perceptions, feelings, and opinions about things within themselves and others. Through this process, the group knows where each member stands and does not need to guess or interpret the meaning of any particular behavior. The more self-disclosure and feedback one gives, the farther down one pushes the horizontal line.

SOLICITS FEEDBACK

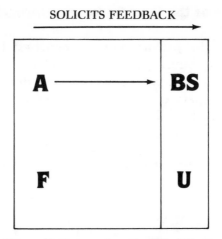

Figure 3. Decreasing the Blind Spot

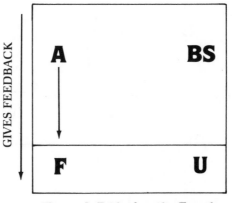

Figure 4. Reducing the Facade

When the Blind Spot and Facade are reduced through the process of giving and soliciting feedback, the size of the Arena, or public area, is increased. However, in the process of giving and asking for feedback, some people tend to do much more of one than the other, thereby creating an imbalance of these two behaviors. This imbalance can have consequences in terms of the individual's effectiveness in the group and the group members' reactions to the individual. The *size* and *shape* of the Arena, therefore, is a function both of the amount of feedback shared and of the ratio of feedback given to feedback solicited.

Characteristics of the Four Styles of Information Exchange

Interpretation of the JoHari Window can best be illustrated by describing four configurations that characterize extreme ratios in terms of soliciting and giving feedback. These descriptions illustrate how people who operate in terms of these ratios might appear to others in a group setting (Figure 5).

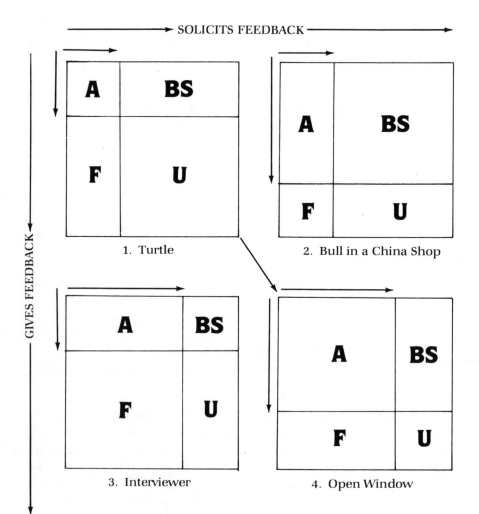

Figure 5. Four Styles of Information Exchange

The Turtle

The first window, with the large Unknown, represents individuals who do not know much about themselves and about whom the group also knows little. They may be the silent members or the "observers" in the group, who neither give nor ask for feedback; thus, for these people, the "soliciting" and "giving feedback" arrows in window number one are very short. Because they appear to have a shell around them, which separates them from other group members, they are called "Turtles." It is difficult for group members to ascertain where they stand with these people or what the turtles' feelings are about themselves in relation to the group. When confronted with their lack of participation, they may respond, "I learn more by listening." Such people obtain very little feedback because their lack of participation provides the other members with almost no data to which they can react. As a consequence, the turtles' opportunity to learn more about themselves and others is reduced.

It takes a considerable amount of energy to maintain an Arena this small in a group situation because of the pressure that group norms exert against this kind of behavior. Energy tied up in maintaining a closed system is not available for self-exploration and personal growth.

Window number one, with the large Unknown, may represent the beginning of a group, when the level of trust is low and group members are engaged in "sizing each other up." As the members develop trust and sharpen their skills in giving and receiving feedback, the large Arena in window number four may reflect this change. The feedback becomes more behavior-based, and a standard of objectivity is established. Furthermore, the standard, however objective, is colored by the mutual concern and caring of the group members.

The Bull in a China Shop

Window number two contains a large Blind Spot. People with such a window maintain their level of interaction primarily by giving feedback—but they solicit very little. Their participation style is to tell the group what they think of it, how they feel about what is going on in it, and where they stand on group issues. Sometimes they may lash out at other group members or criticize the group as a whole, in the belief that they are being "open." For one reason or another, they appear to be insensitive to, or do not hear, the feedback given to them. Frequently, they are poor listeners and respond to feedback in such a way that other group members become reluctant to continue to give it. As a consequence, these individuals do not know how they appear to other people or what their impact is on others. Thus, many of their reactions or self-disclosures appear to be out of touch, evasive, or distorted. The result of this one-way communication (from them to others) is that they persist in behaving ineffectively. Because they are insensitive to the steering function of the group, they do not know what behaviors to change. Their "soliciting feedback" arrow is very short and their "giving feedback" arrow is long. A person with this style of interaction is known as a "Bull in a China Shop."

The Interviewer

The large Facade in window number three characterizes people whose participation style is to ask questions of the group but not to offer information or feedback. Thus, the size of the Facade is inversely related to the amount of information or feedback that comes from these individuals. They respond to the group norm to maintain a reasonable level of participation by soliciting information, e.g., "How do you feel about what just happened?" "How would you have acted if you were in my shoes?" "What is your opinion of the group?" They want to know where other people stand before committing themselves. Their "soliciting feedback" arrow is long and their "giving feedback" arrow is short. Because these individuals do not commit themselves, it is difficult to know where they stand on issues. This style, characterized as the "Interviewer," may eventually evoke reactions of irritation, distrust, and withholding. At some point in the group's history, other members probably will confront them with statements such as "Hey, you are always asking me how I feel about what's going on, but you never tell me how you feel."

The Open Window

The last window is an "Open Window." In a group situation or in any other relationship that is significant to the person involved, the size of the Arena increases as the level of trust increases, and the norms that have been developed for giving and receiving feedback facilitate the exchange. The large Arena suggests that much of this type of behavior is aboveboard and open to other group members. As a consequence, there is less tendency for other members to interpret (or misinterpret) or project more personal meanings into their behavior. This is not to say that this type of person is inappropriately open with people such as casual acquaintances (a behavior that might be seen as threatening) but that in the group or with significant others, most of the person's feelings, perceptions, and opinions are public, so that neither party needs to "second guess" the other.

The goal of soliciting and giving feedback (or of self-disclosure) is to move information from the Blind Spot and the Facade into the Arena, where it is available to everyone. In addition, through the process of giving and receiving feedback, new information can be moved from the Unknown into the Arena. When this occurs, group members may have an "aha" type of experience as they suddenly perceive a relationship between a here-and-now transaction in the group and some previous event. Movement of information from the Unknown into the Arena can be called "insight" or "inspiration" and can result in new behavior (e.g., newly discovered skills, new ways of handling old situations).

Some people feel that giving and receiving feedback cannot be learned solely by practice but require a basic philosophy or set of values that must be learned first. One value that reflects this basic philosophy is that individuals be accepting of themselves and others. As this acceptance of self and others increases, the need to give feedback that is evaluative or judgmental decreases.

REFERENCES

Lewin, K. Frontiers in group dynamics: I. Concept, method and reality in social science: Social equilibria and social change. *Human Relations*, 1947, *1*(1), 5-41.

Lewin, K. *Field theory in social science: Selected Papers.* (D. Cartwright, Ed.). New York: Harper & Row, 1951.

Luft, J. *Group processes: An introduction to group dynamics* (2nd ed.). Palo Alto, CA: Mayfield, 1970.

Luft, J. *Of human interaction.* Palo Alto, CA: Mayfield, 1969.

Chapter 4
Working with Groups

Living in Groups

Among humans, the group is the basic social unit and group living is the predominant mode of existence. Because we are social animals, the majority of human needs can be met only through group life. In fact, many studies indicate that social contact (touching, fondling, affection) is critical to infant survival.

In addition to a primary group (family), most people hold memberships in other groups (e.g., school, work, social, political, or therapy). How effective the person is in each of these groups may depend, in part, on how well the person shifts his or her behavior to meet the required membership standards of each type of group. Considerable tension may occur when an individual must shift role behaviors frequently in order to maintain membership in more than one group, particularly if these shifts in behavior vary greatly between groups. Maintaining behaviors that are appropriate in one group but not in others may cause the individual to be seen as deviant in these latter groups. This is not to say that deviant behavior should not occur in groups; productive discussions and changes frequently occur when new behavior is introduced in a group. Beyond certain limits, however, unfamiliar behavior usually is punished and the individual frequently is ostracized.

If individuals are well accepted by and experience satisfaction with the groups of which they are members, their sense of security and feelings of worth generally are high. If, however, they hold marginal membership in many groups or have difficulty in shifting or adapting their role behaviors to meet the norms of each group, coping and surviving become the primary consumers of their available energy; as a consequence, there is little energy left to engage in personally satisfying or growth-producing activities.

COMMON GROUP ISSUES

Certain issues or concerns are common to all groups, and how these concerns are managed (or mismanaged) are manifested in the group's processes. Underlying group issues is the the basic, universal concern about whose needs are being met—"how much for me and how much for you." Concern for self versus concern for others is the dilemma with which all groups struggle as they attempt to reach a balance between the individual's needs and the needs of the group. This struggle unfolds with many variations as each group attempts to work through the common issues. The issues to be discussed here include goals or goal setting, the management of information, the establishment of group standards or norms, and the development of a group climate in which the members feel accepted and trust one another (see also Gibb, 1964).

Typical "natural" groups include the family, the play/peer group, the school group, and the work group. Examining manifestations of these issues in training groups may aid in the transfer of learnings from the training groups to back-home groups.

Goal Setting

Every group has some purpose for being or attempts to establish one. For some groups, these goals may be very clear; for others, they may be vague. In many natural groups, goals are imposed on the membership through tradition or history; in more temporary groups, goals may be developed by the members. How groups go about achieving these goals, however, may vary—from effective functioning to very ineffective or self-defeating group behaviors. Although the membership in a group may verbally support its goals, the perceived paths to these goals may be quite different; as

a consequence, fighting and competition (or support and cooperation) may develop within the group.

Management of Information

Every group develops ways to handle and process information.
These may include how decisions are made within the group, who
makes the decisions, the determination of whether there is adequate
data for making decisions, and how decisions are implemented.
Factors that influence these processes include the opinions, feelings,
and attitudes of group members; the extent to which people listen
to each other; the areas of information that are deemed acceptable
or not acceptable for discussion and examination; the kind of
information that is expressed directly and openly and the kind that
is censored or withheld; and the people in the group who manage
the flow of information. The nature of problem solving within the
group is highly dependent on the way in which information is
processed. Furthermore, the way in which the group handles
information (e.g., censorship or propaganda) affects the validity of
the data and is critical in shaping the opinions, perceptions,
feelings, and attitudes of the group members.

Group Standards

All groups attempt to manage or control the behavior of their
members by setting standards of behavior and controlling role
functions. Some behavioral standards are explicit—spelled out in
rules, regulations, and policies or passed on by word of mouth.
Many of these standards take the form of norms, which are
supported (wittingly or unwittingly) by the majority of the group's
members and which dictate what behaviors should or should not
take place within the group (see the section on group norms that
appears later). Typical issues include how the group organizes itself
to accomplish its goals, how leadership is handled or accepted,
what role functions are fulfilled, how individuals are made to do
what others want them to do, and what guidelines for interpersonal
behavior are acceptable. Other controls revolve around how group

members relate to other groups and how they handle intergroup issues such as conflict, competition, and cooperation.

Group Climate

All groups attempt to establish an atmosphere that makes them attractive to group members. The issues of trust, belonging, group identity, and mutual support are concerns for every group (see the section on group atmosphere that appears later). But because group members have different attitudes, beliefs, levels of openness, and concerns for their own needs in relation to the needs of others, it is a major challenge to the group to deal with these discrepancies so that they are perceived as assets that enrich the group rather than as problems. How accepted and valued people feel by the group and how free they feel to disagree, be open, and take risks will determine, to a large extent, their commitment to the group, their willingness to support the group's goals, and their willingness to abide by or re-examine the group's standards.

THE THERAPY GROUP

The major difference between therapy groups and other societal groups is that individuals join therapy groups in order to achieve specific personal goals. Membership usually is obtained through a decision by a therapist and the payment of a fee. Maintenance of membership, however, may depend on other factors. The *goal* of the group is to establish group standards or norms and a climate that will facilitate the achievement of individual goals. These may be established by the group leader, developed by the group, or may emerge from the group process. *Information is managed* by the therapist, the members, or both. For example, the therapist makes decisions about when it is helpful to intervene and assesses the readiness of group members to receive feedback; the group members decide when and what they wish to share with others. In contrast to other groups, therapy groups spend a large amount of time *processing* the information that is shared. *Group standards* or norms are set by the leader and group members or may emerge as the consequence of some interaction. Openness (particularly the expression of feelings) and sharing are reinforced by group leaders and by most group members, the exception being when the expression of feelings, particularly negative ones, is seen as threatening to individual members.

In therapy groups, members work to develop a *climate* of acceptance, trust, and support, which is a critical dimension in determining whether or not individual members will share their problems and achieve their goals.

THE HUMAN RELATIONS TRAINING GROUP

Individuals who join a training group have personal goals that they hope to achieve through group interactions and are willing to pay for this opportunity. The *goals* of training groups may overlap the goals of therapy groups in that they both provide an opportunity for individual group members to learn more about themselves, their impact on other individuals in the group setting, some of the dynamics that occur in small groups, and how they affect these processes (Hanson, Rothaus, Johnson, & Lyle, 1966; Hanson, Rothaus, O'Connell, & Wiggins, 1969, 1970). Training groups, however, usually attract or solicit individuals who already are effective in their personal and vocational lives but who may want to *increase* their effectiveness. A further goal of the training group, therefore, is to create an environment in which this kind of learning can take place.

Because the training group is the arena in which the processes that go on in other groups can be studied as they occur in the here-and-now interactions of the group members, another of its goals is to assist individuals to become more effective participants in their back-home groups. For this reason, the training group, as opposed to other groups, pays close attention to its ongoing processes. Here-and-now behavior is examined as it occurs within the individual (feelings, perceptions), between individuals (communication, styles of influence), and among group members (decision making, group norms).

Members are encouraged to express curiosity about personal, interpersonal, and group events. As scientists, individuals will collect data (feelings, attitudes, perceptions), build hypotheses, and test them out with other group members. Thus, through inquiry and sharing, group members can abstract relevant learnings from their experiences.

The focus of attention in the training group is on the development of the group from relative chaos into an effective learning unit. This includes the development of relationships within the group and the identification of personal styles and resources of members. Group members have the right to withhold any personal information not relevant to the goals of the group, and in-depth analysis of individual personalities or back-home problems is discouraged. However, back-home, work-related problems may be discussed when they are relevant to the task or ongoing activity or when meaningful relationships are perceived between what is happening in the group and some back-home event.

Management of information and decision making are achieved primarily through group interaction and group consensus. The goal of group leaders is to facilitate these processes rather than to control them. The expression and sharing of feelings, ideas, and beliefs that are relevant to group goals are reinforced by group leaders and most members. Again, the exception is when individual members are threatened by the expression of feelings and attempt to block this kind of material.

To aid in the setting of *group standards*, training-group leaders frequently act as models to facilitate behaviors that move the group in the direction of openness, exchange of feedback, and risk taking. Other group standards and norms emerge as the result of interactions within the group and the group's assessment of behaviors that facilitate or hinder individual and group progress. Task-oriented behaviors do not receive as much support as do socio-emotional behaviors. As a consequence, group members need to create a balance in which the behavior of task-oriented individuals is seen as legitimate and valued when the demands of the situation require it. The development of group standards and norms to facilitate goal achievement requires continuous monitoring and processing.

The development of a *climate* of trust, acceptance, and mutual support is extremely important in enabling individuals to share their here-and-now experiences. The group's movement toward its goals is not a straight-line progression but vacillates over the period of the group's life. Goals may need to be redefined or clarified periodically, but as long as the group members feel that there is some movement, they generally remain committed to the goals.

Types of Training Groups

In experiential workshops, the basic learning unit is the small group, which usually remains intact throughout the life of the training event. Participants may move out to experience other events in the workshop, but they return to the group to share and process their experiences. Other groupings may be developed from time to time to focus on particular problems, to allow new people to share experiences and consult with one another, and to provide members with fresh perspectives concerning their own behavior and involvement in their primary groups.

The two types of learning groups most often used in human relations training are the group with a trainer (frequently called the T-group) and the group without a trainer (frequently called the D-group).

The T-Group

A typical training group (T-group), originally called a Basic Skills Training Group (Bradford, Gibb, & Benne, 1964), consists of ten to twelve members who meet with a trainer and perhaps a co-trainer and work together as a group for the duration of the training event. The group has no formal agenda, no guidelines concerning appropriate or inappropriate behavior, and no clear-cut leadership. The function of the trainer is to facilitate the efforts of the participants to learn about their own behavior and how that behavior affects the development of the group. Participants also learn about aspects of group behavior such as communication processes, decision making, norm setting, and conflict management.

The trainer does not lead the group or create dependence by directing and controlling group activities. The trainer does provide a model for group members by demonstrating openness, listening skills, and the nondefensive acceptance of feedback. The trainer displays a willingness to accept responsibility for, or "own," his or her own feelings and behaviors and to share personal feelings and reactions with other members of the group. Openness on the part of trainers is an important factor in encouraging risk-taking on the part of the participants. The subsequent openness among group members provides the data around which a learning process can be built. Because the trainers do not provide the type of leadership that participants expect, a leadership vacuum is created and the group members attempt to fill it in order to get the group moving in one direction or another. Their attempts to fill this vacuum become further data for the group to work with. In short, the group's learning experience includes observation and examination of individual members' behavior, how this behavior influences other members, how members' interactions affect and are affected by the processes within the group, and how group members resolve the issue of authority as they attempt to deal with the somewhat ambiguous role of the trainer. Toward the later phases of the group's life, the members begin to assess what they have learned about themselves and other group members through a mutual exchange of feedback.

As group members gain more confidence in handling issues within the group, the role of the trainers becomes less controversial, and the trainers are more free to contribute to the group as "persons" who have some special resources rather than as "leaders." However, although the trainers become more like peers in relation to the other participants as the group develops, they rarely are considered as "just other" group members. By virtue of their assigned roles, the trainers are associated with whatever stereotypes the members may have of the role of "leader"; the effective trainer will use this phenomenon to help participants explore the extent to which their perceptions and reactions are influenced by such stereotypes.

In summary, the T-group represents an arena in which many of the personal, interpersonal, and group events that occur in back-home groups (but are usually not acknowledged or handled) can be confronted and worked through in an atmosphere that enables the participants to learn from these experiences.

The D-Group

The development group (D-group) (Blake & Mouton, 1962; Hanson, Rothaus, Johnson, & Lyle, 1966) is a trainerless or self-directed group and, like the T-group, functions as the major vehicle in a workshop through which learning takes place. In a typical workshop, each of three or four such groups contains eight to ten participants who meet regularly throughout the workshop. Workshops that utilize D-groups tend to have more structure in terms of experiential exercises and theory presentations. Participants are "taught" to run their own groups through structured interventions in plenary sessions and through practice in the use of process instruments. In this respect, the groups are not fully self-directed.

The plenary or general sessions may involve all the groups in the workshop working together on issues that might arise within their groups. For example, the groups may be involved in experiential activities that focus on group-on-group observations; issues of influence, power, or leadership; patterns of communication and participation; and the management of conflict. As the small groups begin to "unfreeze," the members can explore their feelings and perceptions about their own and others' behavior and participation styles, about interpersonal behavior, and about small-group processes. Again, at times the groups may be structured by the staff in the sense that they may be given a specific task; for example, they may be asked to process the activities that occurred in the general session. At other times, the groups will be unstructured, and during these sessions the members are free to do those things that will build their group into a more effective learning unit: build a climate of trust and risk taking, better integrate people into the group, identify and utilize individual resources, develop a process orientation, and establish norms for giving, soliciting, and receiving feedback.

The trainers associated with self-directed groups may specify their roles through a "contract" made with the participants at the beginning of the workshop. This contract generally is stated as follows: (a) the trainers are available as consultants to the small groups; (b) members of a group may invite a trainer into the group, but only if the members agree to do so; (c) a trainer may ask to visit a particular group, at which time the group's members may discuss the request and either invite the trainer in or deny the request; (d) the trainers may be available to consult with individuals as needed.

The Rationale for Self-Directed Groups. The absence of the trainer within the group encourages the participants to take responsibility for themselves in developing a cohesive and effective team rather than becoming dependent on the training staff. Such responsibility tends to create a feeling of ownership and psychological success within the group because the participants feel that "they did it." (This sense of ownership and self-direction can also occur in leader-directed groups, particularly if the trainer facilitates it.) The D-group can provide a significant learning experience when there is a shortage of training staff, and as few as two staff members can conduct a workshop for forty or more participants by dividing them into four self-directed groups. This format creates time for the staff members to prepare for subsequent sessions.

Workshop evaluations have shown that participants have a highly satisfying and "relevant" experience with either group model within a structured workshop (Hanson, Baker, Paris, Brown-Burke, Ermalinski, & Dinardo, 1977). Data collected from a number of workshops in which both types of groups were utilized indicates that the participants' *mean* level of satisfaction and applicability does not differ significantly between the two types of groups.

Table 1. Participants' Mean Ratings of T- and D-Groups[1]

	Satisfaction	Applicability
D-groups (N = 187 participants)	2.7	2.7
T-groups (N = 38 participants)	2.8	2.7
T-groups (N = 19 participants)	2.8	2.5

Support Groups

Support groups are those subgroupings within the workshop (other than T- or D-groups) that are designed to explore special issues within its ongoing activities or special problems that participants bring with them. Support groups serve several functions:

1. They provide a feeling of comfort and encouragement to members from people who are interested in their development.
2. They challenge members by asking significant questions.
3. They provide a small, intimate group with whom members can "touch base" or receive encouragement to try out behaviors in the larger groups.

---

[1]Means based on three-point scale.

4. They handle tasks that would be too cumbersome or time-consuming in the larger groups.
5. They provide members with different perspectives on their behaviors, their groups, and their interactions with others.

Subgroupings Within T- or D-Groups. The basic learning groups may be divided into smaller units (pairs, trios, etc.) in order to more effectively handle issues that are occurring within the groups. For example, the total group may be divided into pairs that are given the specific task of exploring "Where am I in this group?" "Where would I like to be in this group?" and "How do I get there?" The individuals within the pairs would share this information and encourage each other to take certain steps to move toward their specific goals.

If a group is bogged down, the trainer may suggest that the group split in half and that each subgroup diagnose what is going on within the larger group, assess what issues the group is dealing with, and develop a list. This division enables each subgroup to deal with the issues more objectively because the task is similar to diagnosing a "stranger" group. The two subgroups are then brought together to share their lists and look at the similarities and differences. As a consequence of this sharing, the total group may develop a list of action steps to move it in the desired direction.

Participants frequently feel free to bring up an issue in a subgroup with the intention of not dealing with it in the large group. If this behavior becomes a norm, the main group may splinter into cliques or participation may become "flat" and uneventful, with no real work being done. The trainers must stress, in this case, that what goes on in the subgroups must be shared in the total group, and that the subgroups are not to be used to bypass the main group.

Subgroupings Across T- or D-Groups. Subgroups may be created *across* groups to provide linkages through which participants can explore and share issues that they are experiencing within their own groups. For example, if a workshop contained four basic groups, the new groups could consist of two members from each group (or eight members each). The pairing also could be in the form of trios, quartets, etc. This cross-group sharing provides the participants with pictures of what is going on in other groups and with opportunities both to share individual problems they may be having within their own groups and to look at their own behaviors from the perspective of "outsiders." In this way, they may gain new perspectives and new insights about their own groups and their own behavior.

The functions of these new groups may include: (a) trying out new behaviors that have not been tried within the main group; (b) sharing problems that individuals are having within their original groups; (c) developing behavioral goals (as a consequence of feedback from new-group participants) to be implemented in the members' own groups; (d) obtaining feedback (either from new-group members or from original-group partners) about whether or not individuals are meeting their goals; or (e) exploring how learnings from the members' original-group experiences might be applied to their back-home settings. Again, the trainers must remind the participants that the special groups are not established to drain off material that should be handled in their basic groups.

Special-Issue Groups. Groups within the workshop setting can be formed to examine issues that participants have brought with them. For example, same-sex support groups can be formed to explore issues involving sex-role stereotypes and how these affect participation in the groups. Many issues that men or women are reluctant to bring up in mixed groups can be surfaced and explored in these support groups, and participants then may feel freer to deal with these issues in their own groups. In workshops in which there are members who constitute a minority group, but not enough to form a special group, the trainers must be sensitive to minority-group issues as they occur within the basic groups.

The Community Group

The total workshop community provides another learning unit in which individual training groups can share resources and experiences. Workshop settings frequently represent a "cultural island" in which individuals have the opportunity to examine the culture they are creating, the norms they are developing, and how these differ from their back-home counterparts. A major function of the community group is to create a climate in which individuals feel free to surface and share issues that are of concern to them, particularly if they impact the total workshop community.

Groups Within an Organization

Various types of training workshops frequently are sponsored by organizations in order to upgrade the skills of their employees. An external trainer or consultant may be called in to conduct the workshop, or the organization may have its own training staff. One advantage of training conducted within an organization is that the participants may form positive relationships that extend beyond the workshop; e.g., they can negotiate to support each other in what they have learned at the workshop and to exchange feedback on an ongoing basis. Furthermore, if there is a follow-up phase to the workshop, participants can experiment with new behaviors during the interim and bring any problems or issues back to the follow-up workshop. They can then provide mutual consultation on these problems and develop action plans for continued work after the follow-up phase.

Family Groups. Family groups are groups of people who work together within an organization. The family group may consist of workers with equal status or of a supervisor and his or her subordinates. Some managers may be part of more than one family group.

In family groups it may be difficult for the members to be open and to exchange feedback because of the history of their relationships, the norms governing these relationships, and the presence of the authority figure and his or her leadership style. Thus, an important type of training that is generally done with family groups is "team building." (The specific nature of team building is discussed in Chapter 6.)

Cousin Groups. Cousin groups are groups of participants in a training event who are from the same organization but who do not work together within that organization. These people may or may not know each other or know of each other.

FOCUSING ON GROUP PROCESSES

The term "process," as will be obvious by now, refers to *how* people work together, as contrasted to what (content, task, or problem) they are working on. Content issues can be topics that arise outside the group's life, such as member's family or job situations or the effect of the current political system on the economy. Such content issues are referred to as "there-and-then" topics. Other content issues can concern events that are caused by the group and directly related to group activity. These content issues can center around relationships between group members, a task that the group is working on, a decision that the group needs to make, or the development of personal or group goals. While the group is dealing with this content, different members of the group may respond in different ways; feelings of anger may be generated, some members may withdraw, others may attack, and still others may confront the issue more creatively. A few members may increase their levels of participation, become more "alive," and feel more involved and influential. When these events are discussed as they occur, the group is focusing on *process* rather than on task. When the discussion takes place after the process event, the process *becomes* the content. At these times, the distinction between process and content becomes fuzzy. For example, in talking about how outside norms are affecting behavior in the group, the discussion of process becomes the content.

During a discussion of a process (the topic), a process event (here and now) can occur, e.g., when one group member becomes angry with another member who makes an irrelevant intervention. The group members then must decide whether to proceed with the discussion of a process (the content) or stop and focus on the angry interchange between the two members (process). The following examples of content and process statements may help to clarify the distinction.

Member: "My husband says I'm insecure." (content)

Trainer: "How do you feel about that?" (process)

Member: "I could never get a straight answer from my father." (content)

Trainer: "How would you like me to respond to you?" (process)

Member: "I'm always called on to do favors or to give advice. I always seem to be giving and not getting." (content)

Trainer: "Have the same demands been made on you here in the group?" (process)

Member: "Everyone seems so polite here. No one says anything negative, including me." (process)

Member: "It seems as though we never complete a discussion before we jump to another topic." (process)

Member: "At our group session yesterday, I found myself becoming extremely angry at Joan. I know she was withholding her feelings from me, but what puzzled me most was the degree of anger I felt! (a discussion of a process event becomes content)

Trainer: "How do you feel toward Joan now?" (back to process)

One of the major functions of the trainer is to facilitate members' awareness of the group's processes and to aid the members in learning to identify them. Focusing on the dynamics of (what is going on in) the here and now affords group members the opportunity to look at their behavior in a social setting and to assess to what extent they can contribute or do not contribute to that setting. Sensitivity to group process provides group members with a social reality that quite often is missed in everyday living and in back-home groups.

To help a group become more process-oriented, the trainer may want to direct the group's attention to the similiarities between the group as a social system and the culture at large. In this way, the transfer of learning between the two systems can be facilitated.

The training group is a miniature social system in which the members must surface one process issue after another. Thus, process issues concerning goal setting, decision making, norm setting, task and maintenance functions, group atmosphere, and conflict management are dealt with as they emerge in the group.

Participation/Influence

The most important aspect of group process is participation. Without participation there is very little process, and, in most cases, no group. How much a person talks is one indication of his or her involvement in the group. Patterns, styles, and amount of participation provide the basic data on which the diagnosis of other group processes depends. Participation is frequently linked to influence, but they are not the same. High participators may have low influence, and low participators may have high influence. Influence also may be negative—and alienate other group members—or positive—and enlist the support and cooperation of other members. *How* one influences others, then, may be the critical dimension in whether or not people are open to being influenced.

Goal Setting

The goals of the human relations training group have been discussed previously. Setting goals on which group members can agree helps to channel group activity in certain directions and provides a gauge with which groups can assess their progress. If group members differ on the paths to these goals, much of the struggles in which the group engages will involve a search for the "correct" path to accomplish its goals.

Group Standards and Norms

Norms—the standards or ground rules that influence or control organizational, group, or team behavior—are beliefs or desires held or accepted by the majority of people in the group about what behaviors *should* or *should not* take place in the group. Norms can emerge from within the group or infiltrate the group from without (e.g., from the organizational culture in which the group is embedded or from the culture at large). Indeed, norms are one of the most important—and often the most elusive—aspects of organizational culture. This chapter will discuss norms as they relate to the basic group, recognizing that the statements also are applicable to the organization as a whole.

Whether or not a written policy becomes a norm depends on the extent to which it governs behavior. If the behavior of the group members differs from the written standard, then the behavior that is actually practiced is the norm, rather than the written description of desired behavior. For example, if the official policy statement says "staff meetings will begin at 9 a.m. every Wednesday morning" but the staff members usually drift in around 9:15 and the meeting usually starts at 9:30, starting at 9:30 *is* the norm. Explicit norms also may be statements, agreed on by group members, of how the group wants to operate. A standard does not become a norm unless the majority of people in the group behave in accordance with it.

In contrast to formal—or explicitly stated—norms, many norms are *implicit*, that is, very few people are aware of them, but they govern group behavior nevertheless. For example, at every group meeting, members may sit in the same particular seats, in spite of the fact that no seats have been specifically assigned. If one member were to sit in another's "usual" place, the second member would probably become upset and feel that he had been violated in some way. At that point the group might have to examine whether or not the norm was useful.

Implicit norms frequently are not discovered until someone breaks one; and then it suddenly becomes obvious that the group avoids (or engages in) certain topics, interactions, or behaviors. Statements such as "We've always done it this way" and "Don't rock the boat" indicate that implicit norms are operating to which the majority of the members subscribe even though they may not be discussed or explicitly agreed on.

Some norms involving values, beliefs, and behaviors are so ingrained and accepted that they are almost never surfaced or examined. For example, even though group members may be very angry with each other, the question of whether or not to kill each other would probably not be considered an option for resolution of the conflict. Such deeply embedded norms include taboos involving sex, religion, and loyalty to family or institutions.

Norms can either facilitate or hinder group progress or functioning. An implicit norm that says, "the expression and discussion of feelings is not a legitimate area of concern to this group" will hinder group functioning, particularly if the issues with which the group is working evoke strong emotions. Problems arise when an implicit norm is stronger than a stated value or goal of the group or when the values, goals, or beliefs of individual group members conflict with group norms. When this happens, several things may occur: members may pay "lip service" to the group's goals but accomplish little, individuals may exert influence to change the group's goals or norms, members may continue in the group as "deviants," or members may simply decide to leave the group. Whichever force prevails, the result is confusion, lack of direction or commitment, and likely failure to reach either group or individual goals.

Generally, norms serve several purposes. One is goal achievement. In order for a group to achieve a goal, group members must govern and maintain those behaviors that are perceived as facilitating this purpose. Members who do not adhere to these norms will be seen as a hindrance to the group's accomplishing its goal. Secondly, norms are supported if they help the group maintain itself. An intact group does not easily tolerate behaviors that it perceives as having the potential to destroy the group's integrity. Thirdly, in order to maintain itself and to prosper, the group develops norms that increase its attractiveness to team members. Lastly, norms provide a social or consensual reality against which individuals can assess their own realities, e.g., how much they are in touch with the perceptions, judgments, beliefs, attitudes, values, etc., of other group members (or members of their own social group).

The presence of norms is characteristic of all groups, work teams, and organizations. One of the primary tasks for group leaders, managers, and group members is to help the group identify the particular norms under which it is operating and assess their effect on group functioning.

The Here and Now Versus There and Then

One of the primary characteristics of training groups is the focus of attention on what is occurring here and now, both in the group and within group members. This focus is difficult to maintain because people are in the habit of continually dealing with things that happened yesterday, last month, or last year, and planning for things that will happen in the coming minutes, hours, days, or years. In addition, we spend much of our time wishing that things were better or different, desiring this thing or that experience. There seems to be little time in the real world to stop and reflect on what is occurring at the moment. But by failing to develop this habit or skill, people fail to realize, or to admit, much of what they are feeling and choosing.

If a member of the training group is experiencing a feeling that is related to an outside event, her *experience* of that event is "here and now" although the event itself may be "there and then." It is important in this case to encourage the participant to focus on the way *she* is experiencing the event rather than to have her go into a detailed description of the event itself. The "story" of an event usually does not include a description of how the person feels *now*, as she relives the event.

It is a different matter when a participant has a sudden insight about an ongoing experience in the group and can relate or apply that insight to an event or situation outside the group. It is perfectly legitimate at that time to encourage the participant to make the linkage and to describe the nature of the insight and its relationship to the back-home situation—to find a use for the learning.

Most people have difficulty working through here-and-now interactions, particularly when they are of a negative or stressful nature. It is much easier to describe a stressful interaction that occurred yesterday than it is to deal with it competently as it is occurring. The training group is a relatively safe place in which members can learn to handle here-and-now interactions in more effective ways. Because this is the most risk-taking—and, thus, most threatening—part of the group's activities, participants will avoid it whenever possible until a climate of trust and acceptance is developed in the group and they feel able to take such risks.

SOME COMMON PERSONAL/INTERPERSONAL PROCESSES WITHIN TRAINING GROUPS

The observations and experiences described below are derived from a large number of groups and involve issues or ways of coping with personal and interpersonal experiences that are common to most groups. When these issues emerge sporadically or involve group members, the trainer can intervene spontaneously and work with them directly. If an issue appears to be more widespread, e.g., a group norm, the trainer may choose a structured intervention to surface or highlight the issue.

Many of the individual issues that arise in groups are the result of attitudes and coping behaviors that the participants bring with them. These attitudes may reflect resistances to learning, particularly under the conditions of stress that occur when individuals are looking at their own and others' behavior. The ways in which participants handle these threats to their self-images are so common that they can be identified as recurring themes.

Avoiding Interpretation and Cause-and-Effect Hypotheses

The number of ways in which people use the intellect to avoid experiencing things in the here and now is amazing. Much group activity is spent in creating cause-and-effect relationships; whenever an individual group member expresses a feeling, an attitude, or an opinion, other members will begin to conjecture as to why that individual feels, thinks, or behaves as she does. Once a cause-and-effect relationship that sounds reasonable is accepted by group members, further exploration around that experience ceases.

Whenever possible the trainer should suggest to group members that they consider feelings and events simultaneously rather than in terms of one occurring because of the other. For example, in one group a member said, "I am feeling sad because I am thinking of my father." Rather than reinforce the link between the feelings of sadness and the memory of his father, the trainer asked the member if it were possible that "you are sad *and* you are thinking of your father." The member thought for a moment and said that it was very possible. This process allowed the member to focus on his feelings of sadness rather than on his father and to allow other images and memories to occur without stopping to nail one or the other down as the cause of his feelings.

Frequently, the question "why?" starts off a chain of cause-and-effect hypotheses. In a historical sense, this question can never really be answered in the group, and it usually leads to an exposition of different individuals' theories of personality. Even if an event occurring in the group triggers the response, the stimulus is all that truly can be identified, not necessarily the cause.

Statements such as "You made me sad," "You make me feel dumb," or "I am angry because you put me down" usually reflect a belief that other people cause one's feelings and reactions. This places the responsiblity for one's own feelings outside of oneself. The trainer can encourage group members to assume responsibility for their own behavior and its possible consequences or effects on other people but also to assume responsibility for the nature of their own responses to the behavior of others. One particular behavior may elicit different responses in different people—anger in one, amusement in another, and indifference in a third. Although the one behavior may trigger all these different feelings, it clearly is not the cause of any of them.

The feelings that people have generally are carried around with them and are not really new in any situation. These feelings lie just below the surface of awareness, waiting for a particular stimulus to call them up. The causes of these feelings, of course, may lie somewhere in each individual's history, and it is not the task of the training group to explore them. Events similar to those "causes" have the power to trigger those feelings and surface them in response to some here-and-now event. Thus, one's personal reactions may have nothing to do with the other people involved in the interaction. It is important, therefore, to focus one's attention in this learning experience on the feelings, sensations, images, memories, and insights that may emerge within the interaction. For example, group members may become angry with Ann because they feel that she is withholding something from them. In response to this, Ann's feelings may be of irritation or threat and, as a consequence, she may respond defensively. If the ensuing interactions focus on determining who was right and who was wrong, the members may lose the opportunity to explore whatever they felt, sensed, or pictured when they perceived someone as withholding something from them, and Ann may be denied the opportunity to learn what it was in her behavior that caused her to be perceived as a withholding person (and also how she feels about that). It is important in such instances that the trainer not jump into the fray by becoming involved in the *content* of the interaction and that he or she direct the members' attention to the *processes* that are occurring—the nature of the interaction itself.

Interpretations are another way of expressing cause-and-effect beliefs. The professional trainer must be willing to consider all possible interpretations as tentative hypotheses that will alert the trainer to repetitive themes or ongoing behaviors. The trainer also must be willing to consider any evidence that rejects these hypotheses. For example, the trainer may notice that Lee attempts to smooth over a potential conflict by denying the intensity of the negative feelings expressed. The trainer's interpretation of this one event may be that Lee is unable to tolerate negative feelings. The trainer is then alerted to this behavior, and if Lee repeats that behavior several times more, the hypotheses is pretty much confirmed and the trainer can then give feedback on the *observed behavior* (*not* on the interpretation): "Lee, I noticed the last several times (citing the incidents) that when negative feelings were expressed, you came in very quickly to soothe them." The information being given, the trainer allows Lee to choose whether or not to examine the particular behavior. Following the feedback, if Lee does not continue to block the expression of negative feelings, the hypothesis can be dropped along with the issue.

Accepting Responsibility for (Owning) the Consequences of One's Behavior

Sometimes a group member will do or say something (for example, an indirect expression of anger) that triggers negative reactions in another group member. The first group member then may be upset because the second group member is angry or hurt. The attacker may even be surprised and hurt to be responded to so negatively and may counter with, "I guess I shouldn't be so honest in this group." When it is pointed out that the reactions of the second participant appear to be appropriate to the stimulus, the first member may become defensive or make some self-derogatory remark. It frequently is difficult to help some group members to accept the consequences of their own behaviors and their underlying intentions: to hurt the other person.

In addition to expressing angry feelings indirectly, members may engage in other behaviors such as passing judgment on other group members or moralizing about their behavior. These also tend to evoke negative feelings, which may include guilt or remorse at having exposed oneself. For example, if group members are discussing a topic that violates the moral values of an older member, in reaction the older member may say that until these discussions, he really felt a part of the group, but now sees that he is different from the other group members. His statements may evoke tremendous feelings of guilt and defensiveness on the part of the other members. The older member may react to this by stating that perhaps he should leave the group, rather than upset everybody.

It would take a considerable amount of work to assist the older member to recognize the impact of his behavior on the group, to become aware that he was being judgmental by imposing his own standards on others, and to deal with the question "Can I accept other people as they are or are not without demanding that they be different or subscribe to my values?"

We may be so certain that our intentions are honest or well-meaning that we fail to notice that our behavior is incongruent with those stated intentions. The danger in not accepting the consequences of one's behavior is that the "wrong" learning takes place, as in the example above when the member almost left the group. Learning to take responsibility for the consequences of one's behavior is not only a norm that can be established in order to facilitate the examination of human interactions, it is also the first step in learning to examine and modify one's behavior in order to make it more effective.

Re-evaluating Expectations and Demands (Shoulds and Should Nots)

Part of the task of the group is to assist people in looking at their expectations about how the world should or should not be and how other people should or should not behave, particularly in reference to themselves. If one had no expectations of other people or of how the world should be, one would never be upset. It is important for group members to examine the models they have of the world and of their relationships with others to learn to what extent these models are realistic or unrealistic and the consequences that occur when these models are imposed on other people.

People frequently try to shape the behavior of others to fit their models. If they cannot do this, they may terminate the relationship. They then go on to the next relationship with the model intact. When it becomes evident that the next person—be it friend or spouse—does not fit the model, they may again terminate the relationship and keep the model. In other cases, the other person will withdraw from the relationship because that person cannot meet the demands of the model and because he or she has become so defensive that give-and-take interaction has become impossible. Many people go through life clinging to their models and throwing away relationships without questioning the process or the models. The training group provides an opportunity for people to examine their behavioral models and to become aware of the experience of imposing them on others and of having others' models imposed on them. The supportive climate of the group can help members to "loosen up," to shed their unrealistic or narrow expectations, and to accept others as they are. It follows that during this process, they may also begin to accept themselves as they are.

Generating Feelings

Emphasis is placed on the identification and expression of feelings in the group. This includes feelings of apprehension and fear about exposing oneself to evaluation or ridicule by others in the group; feelings of relief or gratitude when a difficult issue is resolved; feelings of anger, hurt, or defensiveness when one receives feedback; and so on. As a consequence of this powerful norm, group members frequently will be frustrated when they cannot "feel." Participants will sometimes try to summon up feelings and be disappointed when they cannot. The trainer can support these people in accepting whatever experience they are having, whether or not it is a feeling. If they are frustrated because they are not experiencing a certain feeling, they can be encouraged to "get into" the experience of the frustration. Even though it is not *the* feeling they are trying to generate, it is a legitimate feeling. In order to experience one kind of feeling they may ignore or miss the feeling that is already present. In getting into the experience of frustration, participants sometimes discover the extent to which they are making demands of and putting pressure on themselves to attain a certain state. Many personal goals cannot be sought directly but are by-products of other goals. For example, seeking happiness directly usually will result in frustration. Seeking to experience any feeling directly may have the same effect. It seems that in the very seeking of the goal, some aspect of ourselves resists and keeps the goal out of reach. This dilemma is expressed in a fragment from Heraclitus described by Rajneesh (1976): "Seekers after gold dig up much earth but find little."

Accepting the Real Person

One thing that participants frequently want to discover during the workshop is "the real me." One frequently hears participants say "What you see isn't the real me" or "I'm really not that way, if only you knew the real me." Angry, defensive, spiteful, competitive, or domineering behavior is often disowned as not being "really me." The "real me" referred to is usually that person in ideal circumstances: when defenses are down, when the person is open, honest, nonjudgmental, and accepting of others. In truth, this ideal person is no more or less real than the person who is behaving in a petty or defensive way. Human beings are complex and are made up of many characteristics, both positive and negative. Part of the purpose of group training is to assist group members (a) to accept their own positive *and* negative characteristics as real for them; (b) to accept this reality without passing judgment on themselves or wishing they were someone else; and (c) to accept this same duality in other people.

Exploring Alternatives to:

The Love/Hate Polarity

Group members frequently believe that because another participant is angry with them, that participant will stay angry with them. There is a tendency to perceive other individuals as having one feeling at a time and as maintaining that feeling until it is replaced by an opposite feeling. Few feelings are so mutually exclusive; although Mary loves Jim, she may also respond with anger to a behavior of Jim's. One may be impressed with another person's accomplishments (awe or respect) and still not *like* that person. Many feelings about other people exist side by side or, at times, with one being more prominent than the other. Such dominance may be only temporary; one feeling may be expressed and then dissipate, its polar counterpart may emerge, or the two may merge and turn into a new feeling. It is important that group members be encouraged to surface and share their feelings, but it is even more important that they learn that feelings are fluid things, that they flow and merge and change in a variety of ways. Such awareness allows one to be more flexible in one's interactions with others and diminishes the fear that negative feelings are more enduring than positive feelings or that one precludes the other. Members can learn that they have a kaleidoscope of feelings to choose from, and this knowledge can increase their behavioral and emotional alternatives.

Keeping Score

Judgmental attitudes about the behavior of others (e.g., right and wrong, on-target or off-target) can preempt alternative ways of looking at what is happening and can severely limit potential learning. The focus of such "scorekeeping" frequently is on the trainer, i.e., members watch the trainer's interventions to see whether or not they are "right on." To be "on target" with these people, the intervention must be meaningful to them, associated with an experience of insight, or (most importantly) in agreement with their own perceptions. These people may indicate their scorekeeping by nonverbal movements such as nodding or shaking their heads or by making statements such as "You really missed that one." When this happens, the trainer can express discomfort at what is going on and make it clear to the group that one person represents only one point of view. The trainer also can ask the group if there is anything in the behavior of the person who is being "scored" that might evoke this kind of response. For example, it may indicate that the person (or the trainer) is intervening too frequently or crowding out the scorekeepers. On the other hand, it may indicate merely that the scorekeepers feel very competitive. Such issues or feelings can then be discussed and dealt with in a more appropriate manner.

Manipulation

Sometimes a member of the group will say something like, "There are some people in the group toward whom I have negative feelings," or "I have been reluctant to give some people in this group feedback," or "I have some special feelings toward some individuals in this group and I'm not sure whether or not I should tell them." This is referred to as the "Last-Supper Syndrome" because the response of others is, "Is it I, Lord?" In most cases the individual fully intends to give the feedback and is merely manipulating the other group members into coaxing it out of him. Frequently, other group members will identify the "game" quality of these kinds of statements and flush the manipulator out into the open. If the statement is an attempt to get the group to engage in one-to-one feedback, but group members do not realize this because the effort is indirect, the initiator may feel disappointed or angry because other group members perceive the attempt as manipulation or because they are not willing to give feedback as "I am doing." Generally, if a group member voluntarily does something such as giving feedback to other group members or taking some risk without an expectation of reciprocal action, other group members may pick up on the activity. If, however, group members discern an expectation of reciprocity on the part of the initiator, they usually will not endorse the activity. This response may not be conscious, and it is important, when it is observed, to surface the process for examination. The fact that individuals try to manipulate the group into doing something does not necessarily mean that the activity would be useless to the group. It is important to identify the way in which action is initiated so that any resistance to the activity can be examined and a more objective choice can be made as to whether or not the group will engage in the activity.

Hanging On

Because we perceive positive feelings to be more temporary than negative feelings (a belief that has not been proved), we try to hang on to them. Having once experienced pleasure, we try to capture it or to repeat the experience. This tendency is particularly prevalent toward the end of a group's life, when the group members have shared many emotional experiences together and are feeling very positive toward one another. Members may express regret at losing the experience (feelings of closeness, belonging) when they go home. At this time the trainer may intervene by saying something like: "This experience has been very meaningful to me, and I will not forget it. I do not, however, want to hang on to the experience or repeat it. Since I created the experience for myself, I want to complete it and create another experience. If this workshop is the only place in which I can create this kind of experience, I haven't learned much. I hope that all of you do not forget this experience, and I sincerely hope that you take with you the courage to let go of this experience and to create new experiences for yourselves."

This kind of statement validates feelings of reluctance to break off from the group and also allows other feelings to emerge (e.g., the desire to leave, feeling good about returning home and sharing the experience) that may have been in conflict with the member's feelings of loyalty to the group. Participants are thus allowed to experience both types of feelings in concert rather than in conflict.

Group Atmosphere

The effectiveness of the group is partially dependent on the climate that exists in the group, which reflects the interaction dynamics among its members and projects a general impression of the way in which the group works. An understanding of what that climate is, how it is produced by group members, and the manner in which it affects their participation can be helpful in identifying ways to make the group more productive.

The group climate may include a number of dimensions at a given time, and these dimensions may shift from one point in time to another. Thus, a group may appear sluggish or tense and then shift to a high degree of work and satisfaction because something occurred to motivate group members to a higher level of activity.

In an atmosphere that is tense, competitive, or characterized by underlying conflict, group members may not feel free to disagree with one another or to express feelings or ideas that may be in opposition to the majority. An increase in conformity and dependent behavior may be evident in group members, limiting their freedom to explore the important issues at hand.

In an atmosphere that is rewarding, cooperative, and work oriented, group members may demonstrate listening, understanding, and supportive behavior and develop higher levels of trust, more risk taking, and greater creativity.

The atmosphere of the group meetings can be identified objectively by the group's members through the use of instruments, or scales, that describe different kinds of group climates. For example, the Group Atmosphere Scales (GAS) (see Chapter 5, page

129) can be completed by the members after each group session, tallies or averages can be compared, and members can then discuss these findings in an attempt to diagnose what is going on in the group.

The words used in the Group Atmosphere Scales originated with Robert R. Blake and Jane S. Mouton (1962) in the 1950s as a check list for groups to consider in evaluating group climate. The scaling of the items and the development of the instrument (factor analysis, etc.) to measure group atmosphere were an outgrowth of research and program evaluation efforts of the Human Interaction Training Laboratory at the VA Medical Center, Houston, Texas.

In completing the scales, each group member rates a group meeting (or series of meetings) on each of nine dimensions that describe impressions or feelings about the climate of the meeting. When grouped, these words can identify more complex facets of group atmosphere that, in turn, can lead to more penetrating diagnoses. The nine descriptions of group climate are:

1. **Rewarding.** When group members have worked well together on a task and the group is satisfied that it has done a good job, a "rewarding" atmosphere will be reported. The group also may feel rewarded if it has accomplished something or made progress on some activity, even though the task is still incomplete.

2. **Sluggish.** Often a group will try quite hard to deal with its task, but "just can't get going." Participation is minimal and sporadic, and the energy level of the group is low. When this occurs, the meeting will be described as "sluggish."

3. **Cooperative.** Group members may work together harmoniously with a minimum of conflict and competition. Group members' contributions build on one another and there is a win-win attitude. When group members share goals and support one another in attaining the group's goals, the atmosphere will be described as "cooperative."

4. **Competitive.** Group members may struggle to have their own points of view accepted by the group to the exclusion of other points of view. The resultant group action is fraught with leadership struggles in a win-lose atmosphere. This kind of interaction will be described as "competitive."

5. **Playful.** The opposite of the task-oriented group is the playful group. This condition exists when a group avoids its tasks

and cannot seem to shake off a light-hearted and frivolous attitude that precludes getting anything done. The bull session can be described as play. Play also can exist in group meetings in which serious work is accomplished, but in an atmosphere of fun and lightheartedness. In this case, the item "work-oriented" also will receive a high rating. An atmosphere of play may also follow a serious session as a way of relieving tension.

6. **Work-Oriented.** When the group devotes itself to its task in a goal-oriented or task-oriented manner, the group atmosphere will be seen as "work-oriented." This may be true regardless of what other impressions are present (e.g., playful, competitive, fighting) and regardless of whether or not the task is completed.

7. **Fighting.** Often group members will find themselves in complete disagreement regarding the topic being discussed, decisions to be made, or action to be taken. In addition, some group members who like an atmosphere of conflict may initiate interactions that are conflict prone. Such "fighting" frequently occurs when there is also an atmosphere of competition.

8. **Taking Flight.** When the group pursues nonrelevant topics as a means of avoiding the real task at hand, the group atmosphere will be one of "taking flight." Taking flight may occur when group members are fearful of surfacing unpleasant or threatening issues; they then will focus their attention on topics that are perceived as safe.

9. **Tense.** When pressures (limited time, conflict between members, or personally threatening topics) are felt, the atmosphere will be described as "tense." Under these conditions, a group may avoid the conflict and take flight, in which case both "tense" and "taking flight" are rated high, or they may surface the conflict and fight. Groups may maintain a tense atmosphere when they do not talk about what is really going on. This is an effort to maintain the myth that if the problem is not addressed, conflict will not occur; when, in reality, the conflict already is present.

These nine words can be supplemented with or replaced by other words such as intimacy, support, suspicion, distrust, trust, and so on. Trainers may want to check their own observations of a group by substituting appropriate words and having the group members rate them.

Decision-Making Procedures

As society becomes more complex and organizations become multifaceted, decisions that affect many lives are rarely made by individuals alone. More and more decision making is done within the context of a group. Adequate decision making requires the pooling of the resources of many people who represent an array of information relevant to the decision to be made. It also requires the identification of alternatives in order to clarify the choices to be made and their possible consequences. These activities are best done within the group context where points of view, feelings, opinions, etc., can be shared, examined, and evaluated.

Whenever groups or work teams meet to accomplish some purposes, some decisions will be made. Regardless of how many members are involved or the nature of the procedure used, these decisions will affect group behavior in terms of subsequent commitment, productivity, and morale.

The following procedures (based on Blake & Mouton, 1962) are used by small groups to make decisions (accidentally or through intent) with respect to topic selection, topic shift, procedures for discussion, or how to handle a task or problem.

1. A **Plop** occurs when someone throws out an idea in the group and the idea is rejected through silence (nobody responds to it and it is passed over). The group, at some level, has made the decision to ignore the idea. If a member plops often, he may become demoralized and withdraw from participation in the group. This effect is based on the belief that *any* response, positive or negative, is usually better than no response. When this happens, it is important for the group members to surface and explore their reasons for not responding to the individual; e.g., the member may be seen as too pushy, his ideas may not be articulated clearly, other agenda may need attention first, or the group simply may not be ready to act on any suggestion.

2. A **Self-Authorized Decision** is made by one individual in behalf of the whole group. The decision even may be carried into action by that one person in order to "get the job done." Alternatives from other group members are not considered, nor is the effect on their feelings given any attention. The self-authorizer eventually

may be overruled or challenged by other group members. On the other hand, members may find it easier to accept the decision than to reject it when they have no ready alternative. Such decisions obviously do not take advantage of one of the most valuable assets of small groups: the pooled and creative thinking of group members.

3. A **Topic Jump** is a technique that groups use to avoid a main issue. Jumping from one topic to another expends group energy and causes a loss of direction. Topic jumps frequently represent self-authorized decisions. They occur when the topic being discussed is not agreed to by all members, when the topic triggers feelings of discomfort, or when there simply is a lack of interest in the topic.

4. A **Handclasp** occurs when one person throws out an idea or makes a procedural suggestion and someone else says, "Go ahead." The *intent* of the person offering the handclasp usually is to support or agree with the person making the suggestion. When group action starts with a handclasp, however, productive ideas from other group members are cut off. The consequences of this procedure are similar to those of the self-authorized decision.

5. **Minority Support** is a procedure similar to the handclasp. In this instance, a minority (less than half) of the group members pushes a decision or suggestion into group action although the majority of the group members may not support it. The majority may be unable to deter the decision because of the force with which the decision is pushed or because of the majority's inability to mobilize its own forces. A minority clique may arrive at a group meeting with prior agreement on a course of action and be closed to influence. The majority may let the decision pass rather than fight it, but there will be little future support by the group as a whole for the action taken.

6. **Majority Support** occurs when more than half the group is in agreement and pushes through a decision. The majority, in the guise of a democratic procedure, may even call for a vote. The major drawback to this process is that it cuts off the flow of ideas by stopping participation and forcing a decision (often premature) to be made on ideas already submitted. In addition, if the minority members have not had a chance to express their points of view, they may feel misunderstood and not support the decision. They

even may attempt to sabotage a decision that they did not help to create.

7. A **Compromise** results when it becomes apparent that group members are not going to resolve or fully agree on an issue as it stands; they gradually move into "give-a-little, take-a-little" positions. Each group member sacrifices something in order to get the job done, but because no one gets what he or she really wants, a climate of uneasiness results. Satisfaction is higher after a compromise than it is as a result of the previous procedures because everyone gets something.

8. **Near Consensus** happens when all members have been given a chance to express their points of view and feel that they are understood, except for one or two members who do not fully agree with the decision but agree to support it. The key to this procedure is that the group has made an attempt to include every member in the debate as well as in the final decision. Support and satisfaction are higher in this case than they are as a result of any of the procedures mentioned previously, but there is always the chance that the dissenting members will hold back at a critical time—such as when the decision is to be implemented.

9. **Polling** does not actually represent a decision in terms of selecting alternative courses of action, but it does help to reach a decision. Polling involves checking with all members of the group to learn their positions regarding an action or decision. This procedure *does not commit* group members to a decision, and further discussion may be held before a decision or agreement is reached. Polling is a way to test for consensus without actually making a decision, although if the polling shows that everyone is in agreement, a decision may be the result.

10. **Consensus** is reached when *everyone is* in agreement. Consensus does not mean that all members agree to pay lip service to the decision; it means that all members think that the decision is the best possible choice of any of the available alternatives. The chance of reaching consensus is increased if all members are involved in the procedures leading up to the decision.

As the size of a group increases, it becomes more and more difficult to reach consensus because more points of view are represented and the dynamics of decision making become more complex. Groups must decide on which issues they need consensus and on which issues other decison-making procedures will suffice. It is important to reach consensus on decisions that bind people to long-range plans, affect their status or influence, or determine how they want to operate as a group. For other kinds of decisions, groups may delegate decision making to committees or accept some behaviors as necessary for more effective functioning (e.g., crisis interventions) or as part of the organizational reality (decisions passed down from above). Even though decisions may be imposed on a group from above, *how* the members implement that decision can be determined by consensus. Again, it is a general rule that people will support what they help to create.

Task, Maintenance, and Individual Role Functions

The behavior of group members is a part of group process that can be described in terms of function or purpose. In any group activity, members assume roles through which they attempt to influence the group—either to accomplish a task, to increase the supportive climate and cohesion of the group, or to satisfy their personal needs. One of the first attempts to identify role behaviors was made by Benne and Sheets in 1948. They identified three classifications of member roles: group task roles, group building and maintenance roles, and individual roles. They also described a variety of functions within each category. Bales (1958) identified first two, and then three, emerging roles: task ("idea man"), socialemotional ("best-liked"), and "deviant" ("not well liked"). Bass (1962 & 1967) also identified similar group roles, which he called self-orientation, interaction orientation, and task orientation. The roles of Bales and Bass appear consistent with Benne and Sheets' groupings. Bass produced the only instrument (the Orientation Inventory) to measure these categories. Bales also developed an interaction process analysis, which is not an instrument but a set of scales that represents a system for categorizing interactions of group members. It is used primarily by trained observers for research purposes.

Task Roles[2]

Function	Description
1. Stating or clarifying the problem or task	Proposing goals and deciding what needs to be accomplished; defining a group problem; agreeing on a specific task.
2. Establishing procedures	Asking for and offering suggestions about the best way to proceed; organizing the group to work on tasks more effectively; agreeing on rules to be followed.
3. Asking for and giving information	Requesting and giving facts, opinions, feelings, and feedback; searching for ideas and alternatives. This may involve going out of the group for resource material or inviting experts into the group to provide information— not for answers to the group's problems.
4. Summarizing	Listing the various things that have been done or said; restating in a clear and brief form the ideas that have been expressed in the group. Summarizing may clarify the status of the group and provide some direction.
5. Keeping the group on topic	Helping the group to remain focused on a particular topic or task; directing the group's attention to the problem at hand.
6. Integrating	Pulling together different pieces of information (ideas, opinions, suggestions) to form meaningful wholes; helping members to build on one another's work.
7. Evaluating	Helping the group to critique its progress, the quality of its decisions, and the effectiveness of its feedback.

[2]See Benne & Sheets (1948) for original conceptualization of group-member roles.

Maintenance Roles

Function	Description
1. Gatekeeping	Bringing silent members into group action; aiding in keeping communication channels open and facilitating the participation of others. (One also can *close* the gate of a talkative member to allow others a chance to speak.)
2. Checking for understanding	Helping people to communicate more clearly, particularly when they are not understanding each other; finding out if everyone is clear on what has been said; clearing up confusion.
3. Giving support and encouragement to others	Accepting or not accepting other people's opinions in a manner that causes them to think about the disagreement and not in terms of personal rejection; encouraging others to express ideas and opinions; being responsive to others; giving empathy and emotional support to others.
4. Helping others to test their assumptions	Checking to see if decisions are made on the basis of irrelevant data or false assumptions and determining whether these ideas or prejudices influence members' behaviors toward one another; testing the feasibility of ideas ("will it work?").
5. Participating-observing	Observing one's own behavior while participating actively in the group and observing the behavior of others in order to provide feedback.
6. Checking for feelings	Facilitating the expression of feelings; asking others how they feel when appropriate and volunteering one's own feelings.
7. Mediating	Attempting to settle disagreements or differences between group members in a constructive way; trying to bring about a compromise if actual differences cannot be resolved.

Individual Roles

Function	*Description*
1. Criticizing	Belittling others, disapproving of their values; not acknowledging the feelings or behaviors of others; devaluing the group and its goals. May involve wit, sarcasm, outright ridicule, or condescension.
2. Obstructing	Preventing the group from moving on by nit-picking issues or challenging every statement; keeping the group "stuck" by means of excessive disagreement or unreasonable opposition.
3. Dominating	Attempting to control the group or the participation of group members by trying to organize or push the group in one direction or another, by taking up an inordinate amount of air time, or by imposing one's own desires or expectations on the group; frequently interrupting others or intervening in interactions between other group members.
4. Seeking attention	Attempting to impress the group with one's special qualities, background, or status; striving to be recognized as someone who deserves deferential treatment by talking about personal achievements, name dropping, or referring to scientific literature.
5. Playing the victim	Calling attention to oneself by appearing "more to be pitied than censored"; criticizing oneself (to avoid being criticized by others); acting confused; or stating one's own personal inadequacies, even when there is no need to do so. This is an attempt to gain support from the group.
6. Playing the playboy/girl	Creating distance between oneself and what is going on in the group by an

	apparent lack of involvement; watering down the importance of the process by means of skepticism or cynicism; kidding around; placing value on activities that conflict with group meeting times or not adhering to the group's schedule.
7. Crusading	Pleading for or against causes or movements in which one is involved; generalizing group issues to the world at large. This strategy keeps the member from dealing with group issues in personal, open, and self-confronting ways and in the here and now; it also may be used to hide interpersonal ineffectiveness by laying the blame for the way one is perceived on someone else's stereotypes.

For a group to work effectively, task, maintenance, and individual functions all are necessary. If a group focuses only on getting the job done, individuals' feelings and their needs to be acknowledged and supported frequently are sacrificed. As a consequence, morale suffers, and the ingredients necessary to maintain the group over time are not developed. On the other hand, groups that are solely maintenance oriented tend to ignore or devalue task behavior and become preoccupied with looking at their processes. As a consequence, the incentive to get the job done is not developed.

One of the many personal variables that a member brings to a group is a set of individual needs (and an expectation that many of these needs will be met). Unfortunately, some of these needs are expressed indirectly or hidden behind well-developed protective behaviors. Maintenance functions are intended primarily to reach the individual at his or her personal need level. If individual needs are ignored, group members may act out these needs in ways that are dysfunctional, and in their attempts to meet their own needs, they may be less sensitive to the needs of others. Such behavior disrupts the group and creates an atmosphere of tension and conflict. This behavior also can energize the group and act as a catalyst for other group members to examine their effectiveness in handling situations in which their own expectations as to how people should behave are violated. Individual-centered behavior is more prevalent in immature groups whose membership either lacks or has not had time to develop or mobilize the necessary skills to create a more group-centered group. As a group matures and there is a more appropriate balance of task and maintenance functions, the dysfunctional, individual-oriented behaviors tend to drop out.

PHASES OF GROUP DEVELOPMENT

It is important that the trainer and the group members be able to monitor and influence the developmental stages of the group. If the choices or interventions made are to influence the group's growth in a positive direction, they must be timed to coincide with or complement the developmental phase that the group is experiencing. Several models of group growth are available (see, for example, Tuchman, 1965). Although the stages are described in sequence and as relatively clear-cut phenomena, this does not imply that group development always progresses in such clearly identifiable fashion. The models that follow can be useful in looking at group development so long as they are not rigidly applied.

Four Stages of Group Development[3]

For purposes of simplicity, we can describe the two purposes or functions of a group as (a) personal relations and (b) task functions. Personal relations refers to the "human" activity that occurs in the group, the development of attachment between the individuals. Task functions involve the development of commitment to the group's task, how people organize to accomplish that task, and so on.

---

[3]This discussion is adapted from John E. Jones, "A Model of Group Development," in J.E. Jones & J.W. Pfeiffer (Eds.), *The 1973 Annual Handbook for Group Facilitators*, San Diego, CA: University Associates, 1973.

Table 1. Stages of Group Development

Stage	Personal Relations	Task Functions
1	Dependency	Orientation
2	Conflict	Organization
3	Cohesion	Data Flow
4	Interdependence	Problem Solving

In groups that are organized to accomplish a specific activity, there are four perceptible stages of group development. Table 1 illustrates these stages.

In the beginning of a group's life, called the *Dependency* stage, individual members must resolve a number of interpersonal issues. They tend to rely on the trainer or group leader to provide structure, set the agenda, and initiate action. Meanwhile, the members become acquainted with the nature of the work they are expected to do. Common behavior includes questioning of why the group exists, what it is to accomplish, how it will accomplish this, and what its ultimate goals are.

In the second stage, interpersonal *Conflict* arises (whether it is surfaced or not) as a result of group interaction as the group organizes itself with regard to task functions. The questions that are dealt with include: Who is going to be responsible for what? What are the work rules? What is the criteria for performance? What is the reward system? The concerns that emerge reflect interpersonal conflict over leadership, structure, power, and authority.

In the next phase, the group has achieved organization and now concerns itself with the flow of data. Personal relations are characterized by *Cohesion* as people experience a sense of belonging to a group and a feeling of catharsis as a result of having resolved their interpersonal conflicts. Members begin to share ideas and feelings, solicit and give feedback, explore actions related to the task, and share information related to the task. This is true even if the "task" of the group is to observe and explore its own functioning.

Frequently during this stage, there is a temporary abandonment of the task as the group members engage in play that expresses their enjoyment of the feeling of cohesion.

In the fourth stage, which is rarely achieved by groups with short lives, the interpersonal dimension is characterized by *Interdependence* and the task dimension is characterized by problem solving. Interdependence means that members can work individually, in any subgrouping, or as a total group. They are both highly person-oriented and highly task oriented. Their activities are marked by both collaboration and functional (positive) competition. The group's tasks are well defined, there is high commitment to common activity, and there is support for experimentation in solving problems.

Cog's Ladder: Another Model of Group Development[4]

The Cog's Ladder model consists of five stages of group development. The first stage is called the *Polite* stage. Because members feel the need to be liked, they spend a great deal of time (whether time is allowed for this or not) in getting acquainted, sharing personal information and values, and categorizing (which may include stereotyping) one another in order to establish an emotional or expectation basis for future interaction. The individual need for approval is high, and the group identity is low. Members avoid controversy and, thus, conflict is almost nonexistent. Nonverbal activities can accelerate the getting-acquainted process during the polite stage.

The second stage is called *Why We're Here* because members begin to ask questions concerning the group's goals and objectives. Some task-oriented members may demand a written agenda, even though this may not be appropriate to the objectives of the group. Cliques may develop among members who find that they have similar personal ("hidden") agendas. All members begin to participate and take more verbal risks.

---

[4]This discussion is adapted from George O. Charrier's lecturette in *The 1974 Annual Handbook for Group Facilitators,* copyright © 1974 by University Associates, San Diego, CA. The lecturette materials are based on Charrier's previous article in the *Advanced Management Journal,* January 1972, 37(1), 30-37.

In the third stage, *Bid for Power*, competition arises. Members attempt to convince the group to take the actions that they believe are appropriate. Conflict is surfaced and struggles for leadership occur. Typical attempts to resolve these issues include voting, compromise, and seeking arbitration.

Team spirit is not felt during this third stage. Rather, some members may feel uncomfortable as hostility is expressed and others will withdraw completely from discussions. Those members who enjoy competition may dominate the group, and cliques take on added importance.

Feedback can be stinging in the Bid-for-Power stage, as the need for general approval declines and members become willing to risk the censure of the group. The range of participation now is widest.

The need for structure is strong, and roles become important as the harmonizer, the compromiser, the gatekeeper, and the follower try to maintain a balance between the needs of the individual members and the needs of the group. Some groups never mature past this third stage.

The fourth, *Constructive*, stage of group development witnesses a change of attitude on the part of group members, who give up their attempts to control and begin to practice active listening. Members become willing to change preconceived ideas on the basis of facts presented by other members and to ask questions of one another. A team spirit starts to build as cliques dissolve and the group perceives that it is making progress toward its goals. Leadership is shared, participation is more even among all members, and conflict is dealt with in a mutual, problem-solving way.

Because group identity is important to members at this point, it may be difficult to introduce new members into the group. Creativity is valued and utilized by group members during the fourth stage, and solutions or decisions are the result of cooperation. Therefore, any structured activity that highlights the values of cooperating, sharing, helping, listening, anticipating group needs, and team building are appropriate for groups to explore in this phase. (Activities that emphasize competition should be avoided because they tend to disrupt group growth and apply pressure to regress to phase 3.)

The trainers can be most effective during the Constructive phase by helping to summarize and clarify the group's thinking, by blending into the group as much as possible, and by refraining from making any comments that tend to reward or punish any group members.

The fifth and final phase of group life is called *Esprit*. It is characterized by high group morale and intense group loyalty. Relationships between individuals are empathic, and the need for general group approval is absent because all members feel approval and acceptance by the group. Both individuality and creativity are high. Members may "agree to disagree," and feelings of freedom and nonpossessive warmth abound.

Cliques are nonexistent in this stage, and group identity may take the form of a symbol or motto. The members participate evenly, and in the learning group (as opposed to the task group) the need for structure disappears. The group is closed to new members at this point, because the integration of new people would require regression to an earlier stage. The group is most constructive and most productive at this point in its life.

Movement from one stage to the next is based on different factors. Any member generally can initiate movement from phase 1 to phase 2 merely by saying "Well, what's on the agenda today?"

The ability to *listen* has been found to be the most important human element in helping groups move from phase 3 (Bid for Power) to phase 4 (Constructive). In some cases, when the majority of group members seem ready to make this transition, the minority of group members who were rooted in the third phase were rejected by the others. However, the transition can be blocked entirely by a very strong, competitive member or clique.

The transition from phase 4 (Constructive) to phase 5 (Esprit), on the other hand, seems to require the unanimous agreement of all group members.

A group will proceed through these five stages only as far as its members are willing to grow. Each member must be prepared to give something up at each stage in order to proceed to the next stage. From phase 1 to phase 2, the members must relinquish nonthreatening topics and risk the possibility of conflict. Between phase 2 and phase 3, members must put aside a discussion of the group's purpose and commit themselves to *some* action, risking personal attacks in carrying out that action. Growing from phase 3 to phase 4 requires that individuals risk the possibility of being wrong and display some measure of humility. The final move to phase 5 requires that members trust themselves and other group members and are willing to risk the consequences of that trust.

REFERENCES

Bales, R.F. Task roles and social roles in problem-solving groups. In E.E. Maccoby, T.M. Newcomb, & G.L. Hartley (Eds.), *Readings in social psychology*. New York: Holt, Rinehart and Winston, 1958.

Bass, B.M. *The orientation inventory: Manual* (research ed.). Palo Alto, CA: Consulting Psychologists Press, 1962.

Bass, B.M. Social behavior and the orientation inventory: A review. *Psychological Bulletin*, 1967, *68*(4), 260-292.

Benne, K.D., & Sheets, P. Functional roles of group members. *Journal of Social Issues*, 1948, *4*(2), 41-49.

Blake, R.R., Mouton, J.S., & Sloma, R.L. The union-management intergroup laboratory: Strategy for resolving intergroup conflict. *Journal of Applied Behavioral Science*, 1965, *1*(1), 25-57.

Bradford, L.P., Gibb, J.R., & Benne, K.D. (Eds.). *T-Group theory and the laboratory method*. New York: John Wiley, 1964.

Ermalinski, R., Hanson, P.G., & O'Connell, W.E. Toward resolution of a generation gap conflict on a psychiatric ward. *International Journal of Group Tensions*. 1972, *2*(2), 77-89.

Gibb, J. Climate for trust formation. In L.P. Bradford, J.R. Gibb, & K.D. Benne (Eds.), *T-Group theory and laboratory method*. New York: John Wiley, 1964.

Hanson, P.G., Baker, R., Paris, J., Brown-Burke, R.L., Ermalinski, R., & Dinardo, Q. *Training in individual and group effectiveness and resourcefulness: A handbook for trainers*. Washington, D.C.: Department of Medicine & Surgery, Veterans Administration, 1977.

Hanson, P.G., Rothaus, P., Johnson, D.L., & Lyle, F.A. Autonomous groups in human relations training for psychiatric patients. *Journal of Applied Behavioral Science*, 1966, *2*(3), 305-324.

Hanson, P.G., Rothaus, P., O'Connell, W.E., & Wiggins, G. Training patients for effective participation in back-home groups. *American Journal of Psychiatry*, 1969, *126*(6), 857-862.

Hanson, P.G., Rothaus, P., O'Connell, W.E., & Wiggins, G. Some basic concepts in human relations training for psychiatric patients. *Hospital and Community Psychiatry*, 1970, *21*(5), 137-143.

Rajneesh, B.S. *The hidden harmony: Discourses on the fragments of Heraclitus.* Poona, India: Rajneesh Foundations, 1976.

Tuckman, B.W. Developmental sequence in small groups. *Psychological Bulletin*, 1965, *63*(6), 384-399.

Chapter 5
The Use of Instruments and Structured Activities

AN INTRODUCTION TO INSTRUMENTATION

Most people have experienced meetings in which work on the agenda becomes bogged down; people fail to pay attention, jump from topic to topic, or nitpick on issues not pertinent to the agenda; and the atmosphere becomes sluggish. The usual strategy in these kinds of meetings is to continue to grind out the task in hopes of accomplishing it or, for those in the leadership role, either to make decisions for the group or to postpone the agenda. Very seldom do groups stop the action, put aside the agenda, and look at *how* they are working or *what* is going on in the meeting. Individuals rarely state how they are feeling about a meeting (e.g., "I'm feeling bored and tense right now," "I am really upset with the way this meeting is going on.") These comments have to do with here-and-now interactions and feelings rather than with content.

In most work groups, and even in many therapy groups, norms do not exist to encourage members to examine these dynamics. Such behavior may be seen as not relevant to the agenda or group goals or, at worst, as destructive to group functioning. Some attention to how the group is working (process), however, may enable group members to (a) understand why they are bogging down and (b) proceed more effectively with the task. Even though norms do not exist to enable group members to spontaneously comment on how the group is working, a simple questionnaire involving questions or scales can encourage the group members to begin looking at their own process. If group members think of themselves as *studying* their group through an "objective" instrument, the activity seems more scientific, less subjective, and more acceptable.

Instruments are paper-and-pencil assessment devices (questionnaires, surveys, rating sheets, etc.) that extract information organizational use, they frequently are referred to as survey-feedback designs. In a group without a leader, an instrument can be used to put the responsibility for processing the group's activities on the members themselves. Instruments also can be used in more structured workshops to familiarize the participants with the use and value of instruments in processing their workshop groups, in the hope that the participants will transfer these skills to their back-home groups. Lastly, instruments can be used in work teams and meetings to evaluate their effectiveness.

The use of instruments to identify processes that are occurring in the group can serve several purposes.

1. Instruments facilitate the focusing of attention on dimensions of group behavior that might otherwise be missed by group members. In addition, an instrument provides a process orientation.
2. Instruments objectify individual impressions through group tallies or averages of the items of group behavior being diagnosed. They provide a measure of social reality of group behavior through the collective perceptions of group members and allow group members to check their perceptions against those of others.
3. They can provide structured and "objective" feedback to the group concerning ongoing events, what the here-and-now status of the group is, what the members would like it to be, and how far the group would have to go to get there. Groups also can track their own progress over time and compare their performances with other groups.
4. For new or inexperienced groups, the use of instruments is a relatively unthreatening way to obtain group data. Instruments lend an air of objectivity and scientific inquiry to the group's discussion of its own dynamics and provide the necessary "distance" for group members to be involved

and, at the same time, to stand back and look at their own behavior.

5. The use of instruments develops a feedback norm that encourages groups to collect more data about themselves.
6. Instruments provide a teaching device to acquaint group members with a variety of group behaviors and to give the staff information to plan group interventions.
7. Instruments can provide data for research purposes. Qualitative items can be quantified and subjected to statistical analysis.

Instruments designed to measure or highlight facets of group behavior and the behavior of individuals in groups range from those on which considerable work has been done in terms of reliability, validity, and normative data to those that are developed on the spot to stimulate discussion and feedback. Many instruments are developed from theories of personal and group behavior such as leadership styles (Blake & Mouton, 1964; Burke and Hanson, 1976), interpersonal needs (Leary, 1957; Schutz, 1978), and group role behavior (Bales, 1970). For review and assessment of instruments measuring a variety of personal, interpersonal, and group behaviors, see Lake, Miles, and Earle (1973) and Pfeiffer, Heslin, and Jones (1976).

A number of group dimensions can be assessed through the use of the instruments that appear in this chapter. Some of these instruments originated with Robert Blake and Jane Mouton and were modified and further developed by the Human Interaction Training Laboratory at the VA Medical Center, Houston, Texas.[1]

---

[1]The format for the Participation Scale, the Group Member Evaluation (GME), and the Group Behavior Questionnaire originated with Robert Blake and Jane Mouton, Scientific Methods, Inc., Austin, Texas. In May 1961, Robert Morton, then chief of psychology service at the VA Hospital in Houston, set up the first human interaction training laboratory (HITL) to be used with hospitalized patients. Blake and Mouton, then at the University of Texas and consultants to the patient training laboratory (PTL, later changed to the HITL), provided the design of the laboratory (instrumented laboratory with self-directed development groups) and most of the instruments used. Since that time we have modified or replaced much of the content of the instruments and changed the scoring procedure in the Group Behavior Questionnaire. The author expresses appreciation to Blake and Mouton and to Morton.

All the instruments were designed to assess the important aspects of group functioning described previously in this book.

Administering Instruments

The format and content of an instrument will depend on the proclivities of the designer and the factors that the instrument is intended to measure. Attractiveness, clarity of format, and ease in responding or scoring are important aspects of instrument construction and facilitate the cooperation of group members in completing the forms. It is important to go over each instrument thoroughly with the participants to make certain that they understand the instructions and the definition of the concepts to be assessed. It is also wise to stress that the instrument is not a "test" but is designed to present the group with a picture of some aspect of itself.

The question of whether or not participants should identify themselves on the instrument has several answers. If the participants feel anxiety about self-disclosure (as they might in a work setting), a more truthful response may be obtained if the responder remains anonymous. Even participants in a training laboratory may "pad" their ratings because they fear group rejection. In such cases, members may be asked to code their forms (using part of their social security numbers or phone numbers, for example) so that they can be identified later by the respondent only and retrieved for the discussion of the items that were scored. In any case, the trainer should reinforce norms of openness and honesty in filling out the forms and, if appropriate, should also encourage group members to "own" their responses (identify themselves).

It is important that the person administering the instrument not give the respondents "clues" about how he or she wishes them to respond (in terms of content) to the items. It is also important to stress that members should answer each item as honestly as possible.

Designing Instruments

In constructing instruments that are composed of scales, the number of points on a scale, how many points are described (labeled), and the clarity of the items are of primary importance. Some people prefer to use an even number of points on a scale, based on the assumption that the respondents will be forced to select a rating either above or below the nonexistent middle point (the choice point for people who want to play it safe or who do not want to make the effort to discriminate). On the other hand, not having a midpoint may force a respondent to ignore a reality that he or she actually perceives. Having too few points on a scale does not allow much discrimination. Having too many points may give the false impression that the item is so refined that the number of choices is justified. In making such choices, the designer must use his or her own judgment in terms of the purpose of the scale, the clarity and specificity of the behaviors or events to be rated, and the face validity of the items in assessing the behaviors to be examined.

The number of points on the scale to be labeled will depend on the trainer's and/or group's needs for greater or lesser reliability. The more points that are labeled, the easier it is for group members to rate them with reliability. This greater reliability, of course, would be important primarily if the scales were to be used for research purposes. In labeling a scale, it also is important not to use words that change the concept of the original item. For quick assessments to help groups process their meetings, the designer may choose to label only the two extremes of the scale.

The last issue in designing scale-type instruments, clarity of the item (behavior or concept described), is extremely important if all group members are to make choices from the same frame of reference. Even sophisticated designers will sometimes contaminate items so that the results may be difficult to interpret. A frequent contamination occurs when more than one dimension is mentioned in one scale, e.g., "To what extent are group members *participating* and *involved?*" In this example, *participating* would refer to the amount of talking while *involved* would be an interpretation of participation. Another example of contamination is mixing the scale with the item: "Are participants *highly* involved?" rather than "How involved are participants?" Specificity lends clarity to an item. An item such as "To what extent are norms operating in the group?" is too general and not very meaningful, whereas questions such as "How often is affection expressed in the group?" (on a scale of "not at all" to "very frequently") and "How is conflict handled by the group?" (on a scale of "avoided" to "openly confronted") will identify norms in a more specific and meaningful way.

It is also helpful to word items so that the answer can be graded on a continuum rather than discretely. For example, a scale that measures *degrees* of managerial control (high control, some control, little control, no control) results in a continuum; whereas on an instrument that identifies sources of managerial control (fear, threats, punishment, etc.), the items must be graded discretely; i.e., individually. A continuum generally is indicated by the use of adjectives or adverbs (high-low, often-not often, moderate-very much), and discrete items generally are nouns or verbs (reward, punishment; does, does not). Unfortunately, some designers use discrete items as if they were a continuum.

The Reliability and Validity of Group Instruments[2]

In considering the reliability and validity of group instruments, one is faced with the choice of using standard but often irrelevant tests of proven reliability and validity or of developing new instruments that have relevance to the specific behaviors and attitudes one is seeking to study or change. For any instrument to have value for research, it must be developed with appropriate concern for its reliability and validity. Even if the data from the instrument is to be used to stimulate discussion in small groups, it must be reliable and valid so that the group members share a common understanding of what is being discussed.

If instrument data is to be discussed by group members, the reliability and validity of the instrument is best developed not with external raters or judges, but with group members as raters, because the determinations of external raters may not be the same (in terms of meaning) as those of group members to the same items. Frequently, training programs can be structured to have group

[2]Appreciation is expressed to Dr. Rodney R. Baker, research consultant to the Human Interaction Training Laboratory, who worked with the author on this section and who conducted these instrumentation studies. Dr. Baker is now chief of psychology service, VA Medical Center, San Antonio, Texas.

members do for themselves what staff members or external consultants would do for groups in other settings.

Test-retest reliability generally is not a factor in small-group research, because changes over time in item scores are *expected* and desired as a result of changes or growth in personal and group behaviors.

Still another issue for all research efforts is the fact that a perfectly reliable score may require the measurement of a variable that is so discrete and simple that it has little or no value or meaning. Let us take "participation" as an example. The amount of participation by each member of a group is unquestionably a crucial group variable. If participation is defined as the number of words spoken by a group member during a session, one could measure that dimension perfectly by attaching a microphone to every member and calculating the number of words spoken by each member. Granted that there are some research designs in which such information is desired, the limitations of such a measure for use in small-group discussions is obvious. The number of words spoken provides almost no information for group members; they are more interested in the quality, nature, or impact of the words spoken. Most important issues in social living are heavily laden with such value judgments. Thus, whenever all members of a group find agreement easy in rating some dimension, the information obtained and the potential for important learnings may be limited. The other side of this coin is that if reliability is very low, it may be an indication that the items to be scored are not clear to the respondents. Obviously, a balance is required in order to satisfy both legitimate research obligations and the goals of a training program.

Equally important to considering group variables that can be rated with some consistency is the question of validity: *what* is it that the group members are rating? For example, when group members rate each other on "participation," it may be difficult to ascertain how much they are rating quantity of talking, as opposed to other factors such as influence and leadership. It is not sufficient to assume that because a group dimension such as participation is being rated reliably (group members produce the same score), the members are in agreement on exactly *what* they are rating. Although an instrument may have face validity (informal agreement among investigators on the definition of terms), the question of whether or not the instrument is measuring what it is supposed to measure should be subjected to experimental studies specifically designed to provide construct validity. A minimum effort to establish such validity is to review the dimensions with the group members prior to their ratings to make certain that everyone is in agreement about the definitions of the dimensions. The focus—as was the case with reliability measures—is whether or not the *group members* understand the items, not whether external raters or judges agree on the dimensions, since they may agree for reasons other than those of the group members. It is the group members after all, who will complete the ratings.

SAMPLE INSTRUMENTS

The Group Atmosphere Scale

The Group Atmosphere Scale (GAS) is a brief, nine-item assessment instrument that can be used to identify the climate or atmosphere of any small group with a task to accomplish.

It can be used after a group meeting to assess the meeting. The trainer should define all words on the form to make certain that the members understand them and will be rating them from the same frame of reference. Each member then circles the number on each scale that best describes the atmosphere of the meeting as he or she experienced it.

Each of the items on the GAS are scaled for four degrees of intensity. The ratings are then transferred to the tabulation sheet and group averages are computed. The individual ratings and averages provide data for group analysis and discussion. It is important not to lose sight of the individual ratings, particularly if they are consistently more negative than the group's average. These ratings may reflect feelings that need to be acknowledged and worked through. Once the members have identified the climate in which the group is working, (e.g., as one of tension, flight, play, etc.), group members can examine their own feelings and inter-actions to discover the underlying elements that are contributing to this atmosphere.

In using the GAS, group members rate elements of each group session as rewarding, taking flight, tense, playful, work-oriented, etc. The group computes averages for each item and can plot this on a day-by-day scale. Thus, group members can look at the daily atmosphere of their sessions as seen by each group member. It also can help to identify the factors that facilitate or interfere with the work of the group. For example, some group members might indicate the impression that not much work was done at a particular meeting because of a lack of interest or a low level of energy. The impression might exist among others that a lot of work was accomplished but that, in the course of work, tempers flared or members were "edgy" or "touchy." The identification of these impressions and a subsequent discussion of what produced them can assist the group in determining what actually occurred in the meeting and what might be done to make such meetings more effective. If group or team sessions are recorded, these recordings can then be analyzed in terms of the interactions that contributed to group members' perceptions of the atmosphere, as reflected in the scales.

Data from the Group Atmosphere Scales also can be related to other group diagnostic instruments (e.g., Gibb, 1977) that measure such things as how open members feel, the level of trust, how the group makes decisions, how the group handles feedback, and how the group manages conflict.

Interjudge reliability studies (Baker, Hanson, & O'Connell, 1972) were made with twenty different work groups (N = 207 hospital personnel) to determine the extent of agreement among members in each group in the rating of the GAS. An intraclass correlation coefficient was used to assess the interjudge reliability for all nine GAS words.[3] The estimated reliability for the mean of the ratings given by all group members ranged from .85 to .97, with the exception of one group whose coefficient was .60. Reliability coefficients for individual raters also were computed, and these ranged from .38 to .85 for all groups, with seventeen of the twenty groups having .54 or greater. Again, Group 8 was an exception, with a coefficient of .12. The standard error of measurement of the mean for each word also was calculated for each group, and these ranged from .12 to .22. The relatively small standard error of the

---

[3]The words used in these studies were: rewarding, sluggish, cooperative, competitive, play, work, fight, flight, and tense.

mean and the high rater-reliability coefficients suggest that group members, as judges, have little difficulty in agreeing on the measurement of the GAS words.

The same nine group-atmosphere words have been factor analyzed on several patient and nonpatient populations (280 school administrators, 328 teachers and community leaders). Two factors emerged consistently: *satisfaction-productivity* (loaded as to rewarding, work, and not sluggish) and *tension* (loaded as to tense, fight, and flight), with a third factor (play) being somewhat variable. Attempts to replicate this factor structure with the laboratory patients have not been successful up to this point. The above factor structure is noted at certain times during the four-week program, but at other times the structure of the factors vary. The participant's interpretation of or reaction to the *play* variable, for example, takes on different meanings at different times during the program. At times play is related to or interpreted by the participant as an avoidance of work or conflict and at other times it appears to have an identity of its own, i.e., not related to work or conflict.

Data from these studies (Baker et al., 1972) also suggest that early in the group's life, before the trust level is high, groups avoid or handle *tension* and potential conflict by *taking flight* or *playing*. Later in the group's life, when norms for feedback and confrontation are established, group members deal more directly and openly with tension and conflict (less flight and play). In addition, for one data group, "competitiveness" is more important in determining the tension factor than it is for another group, in which "flight" is more important. When the factor and individual-word data are compared with other measures of program success, it is the satisfaction-productivity score that is more often related to program-success data; the level of tension in a group is relatively independent of most program-success data. The factor analyses to date, however, suggest that the satisfaction-productivity factors and the tension factors are rather stable over the different populations and that these factor scores can be calculated and used to condense the information contained in the nine atmosphere words, e.g., the satisfaction-productivity factor covers "reward," "work," and "not sluggish," and the tension factor includes "tense," "fight," and "flight." "Play" was variable.

Two other scales can be used with the GAS or independently. These are concerned with the here-and-now interaction in the group and the openness in the group. Both of these concepts should be defined for group members so that they understand—and have some agreement on—what they are rating. The term "openness," in particular, tends to be value laden, and people differ in their definition of it.

Here and Now

The Here-and-Now Scale measures incidents or processes that occur within the particular group session that is being rated. That is, "here and now" refers to what is going on in the group in the present, as opposed to "there and then" back-home problems, past events, or workshop events that are outside the group.

The Here-and-Now Scale helps the group to focus on what is happening in the group "now." This orientation is based on the belief that if members can learn to deal with their feelings as they emerge, they will be better able to manage their feelings in the future. In addition, the Here-and-Now Scale emphasizes the essentially nonhistoric character of human relations training programs.

Each group member circles the number on the scale that best reflects that member's perception of the locus of discussion of the group for most of the group session. These ratings are then transferred to the tabulation sheet, and a group average is computed.

Openness

At the end of a group session, each member also may rate the extent to which he or she felt "open and frank" during the session. These self-ratings can be averaged to provide an indication of how open or closed the whole group felt during that particular meeting. Individuals far below or above the group average may contribute highly individualized data that might have been missed otherwise. The Openness Scale also helps individuals to identify sources of threat or barriers to being open and taking risks.

The Openness Scale is extremely important because of the strong tendency of people to suppress their problems by putting on a front and masking their feelings. There are powerful norms in our culture against expressing feelings, particularly negative feelings. As a consequence, hidden feelings or behaviors become barriers to more effective interpersonal relationships. Being open helps to clear the air so that more constructive interactions can take place, and openness tends to elicit openness. It is a two-way street; when one is open toward others, they may be encouraged to be open as well. In addition, openness in giving feedback enables the recipients to take more honest looks at their own behavior and how that behavior affects their relationships. The group setting can be an extremely useful place in which to try out more open behaviors because the group norms (as opposed to the back-home norms) support this kind of expression.

Group members circle the number on the Openness Scale that best describes their perceptions about themselves in terms of how open or closed they felt during the group session. These ratings can then be transferred to the tabulation sheet and the group average can be computed.

When used in conjunction with the GAS, the Here-and-Now and Openness Scales enrich the picture of what is happening in the group. The Openness Scale is a rating of one's perception of oneself, whereas the other scales are based on one's perceptions of the group. It is important, therefore, to note individual group members' ratings on the Openness Scale, particularly those members who felt very "closed." When the data from these scales are surfaced in plain sight, the group members can explore the underlying dynamics that contributed to the ratings.

It is important to stress to members that the real value of the scales (as with any other instruments) is the stimulus they provide for group analysis and discussion. Through this discussion, members can identify feelings, perceptions, or opinions that are related to counterproductive motivations and underlying dynamics that may be blocking group decision making or productivity.

GROUP ATMOSPHERE SCALE

Name: ——————————————————————— Date: ———————————

I felt that the meeting was: (Circle *one* number on each line.)

Rewarding	4 Very	3 Somewhat	2 A little	1 Not
Sluggish	4 Very	3 Somewhat	2 A little	1 Not
Cooperative	4 Very	3 Somewhat	2 A little	1 Not
Competitive	4 Very	3 Somewhat	2 A little	1 Not
Playful	4 Very	3 Somewhat	2 A little	1 Not
Work-Oriented	4 Very	3 Somewhat	2 A little	1 Not
Fighting	4 Much	3 Some	2 A little	1 No
Taking Flight	4 Much	3 Some	2 A little	1 No
Tense	4 Very	3 Somewhat	2 A little	1 Not

Here-and-Now Scale

To what extent did we talk about events arising out of our group's activity (here and now), and to what extent did we talk about events not caused by group activity (there and then)? (Circle *one* number.)

9 Completely here and now

8 Almost completely here and now

7 Quite here and now

6 Somewhat here and now

5 Equally between here and now and there and then

4 Somewhat there and then

3 Quite there and then

2 Almost completely there and then

1 Completely there and then

Openness Scale

Was I open with the group? That is, did I feel free to say what I really thought and felt at the time I felt it was necessary, or did I find it impossible to express my true feelings?

I felt: (Circle *one* number.)

9 Completely free and expressive, open and above-board

8 Almost completely open

7 Somewhat open

6 Slightly more open than closed

5 Neither open nor closed

4 Slightly more closed than open

3 Somewhat closed

2 Almost completely closed

1 Completely under wraps, closed, and hidden

Group Atmosphere Scale Tabulation Sheet

Group _____

Date _____

Group Atmosphere Scale

		1	2	3	4	5	6	7	8	9	10	11	12	Total	Avg.
Rewarding	9														
Sluggish	8														
Cooperative	7														
Competitive	6														
Playful	5														
Work-oriented	4														
Fighting	3														
Taking Flight	2														
Tense	1														

Here-and-Now Scale

1	2	3	4	5	6	7	8	9	10	11	12	Total	Avg.

Openness Scale

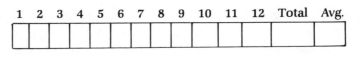

1	2	3	4	5	6	7	8	9	10	11	12	Total	Avg.

The Group Member Evaluation: Identifying Roles

The Group Member Evaluation (GME) is a rating scale and also a feedback instrument describing group-member activities that are translated into task, maintenance, and individual role behaviors. Group members are asked to rate themselves and others on each of the fourteen items, using the seven-point scale.

Before filling out the forms, each group member should be assigned a *number* (this can be done by numbering the group roster in alphabetical or some other order, e.g., Alice becomes member 1, Breck becomes member 2, and so on). These numbers are then used to identify the members on the rating sheets, i.e., member 1 would rate members 2, 3, 4, etc. After completing the ratings of their peers, the members rate themselves *as they would like to be* (ideal self). The ratings are then shared by group members in a feedback session and are transferred to the summary sheets for each individual. This procedure may be reversed, in which case the summary sheet would be distributed first, the ratings would be shared in the feedback session, and each group member would record the ratings that others made of him or her on the summary sheet. The ratings for each item are totaled and averaged for each group member. This process allows each member (member 1, for example) to look at all the ways the other members rated her, to see if these ratings are consistent across any dimensions, and to compare her self-rating with the *averages of the group's ratings* (mean-other rating).

Obviously, feedback instruments such as this cannot be used until the group members have had sufficient exposure to one another to enable them to make these ratings or until they are familiar with the terms used in the items to be rated. Three-to-five days of group meetings generally is ample time for group members to collect this type of data about one another. The items on the scale have been factor analyzed and reflect group activity (task and maintenance), alienation (individual orientation), and talk. (The original instrument, used in the factor analyses, contained two additional items: "Talks about his medical problems" and "talks about his psychological problems," and was rated on a nine-point scale.) For research purposes, factor scores can be assigned to individual group members.

Other items can be substituted in the GME format to suit the goals of the training group, e.g., to identify some of the more typical task and maintenance functions rather than the individually oriented ones. It should be noted that the factor analysis described here applies only to the original instrument; some items, as noted previously, have been changed to adapt the instrument for general use.

Functions		Team Roles
TASK	1	Asks for and gives information
	2	Helps to define and clarify the task
	3	Suggests procedures or ways to handle the task
	4	Keeps the group on target (task or topic)
	5	Pulls together (integrates) ideas, opinions, suggestions, etc.
	6	Summarizes discussion or activities in the group
MAINTENANCE	7	Encourages others to participate
	8	Gives support and encouragement to others
	9	Checks to see if self and others are understood
	10	Expresses own feelings and checks for feelings in others
	11	Mediates differences or tries to reach compromise
	12	Gives feedback to and asks for feedback from others

Figure 1. Team Roles

Group Member Evaluation (GME) Rating Sheet

Group _____   Name (or Code) _____

Date _____

Circle One: 1st time   2nd time

Items	| Group Members by Number												Ideal Self
	1	2	3	4	5	6	7	8	9	10	11	12	
1. Expresses him/herself clearly.													
2. Levels with other members.													
3. Provides helpful feedback to other members.													
4. Takes lead in selecting topics and procedures.													
5. Helps other members express their ideas and feelings.													
6. Helps group to stay on target.													
7. Annoys others.													
8. Sets him/herself apart from the group.													

| | Group Members by Number | | | | | | | | | | | | Ideal |
Items	1	2	3	4	5	6	7	8	9	10	11	12	Self
9. Is hard headed, sticks to his/her point regardless of feedback.													
10. Runs away when faced with a problem; goes into flight.													
11. More ready to fight than to work out problems.													
12. Dominates and imposes his/her will on the group.													
13. Pays attention to what other group members have to say.													
14. Is warm and friendly.													

Rating Scale: 7=Always; 6=Almost always; 5=Fairly often; 4=Sometimes; 3=Not too often; 2=Almost never; 1=Never.

Group Member Evaluation (GME) Summary

Group _____   Name (or Code) _____

Date _____

Circle One: 1st time   2nd Time

Items															Own Ratings		
															Total	Avg.	Own Ideal Self
1. Expresses him/herself clearly.																	
2. Levels with other members.																	
3. Provides helpful feedback to other members.																	
4. Takes lead in selecting topics and procedures.																	
5. Helps other members express their ideas and feelings.																	
6. Helps group to stay on target.																	
7. Annoys others.																	
8. Sets him/herself apart from the group.																	

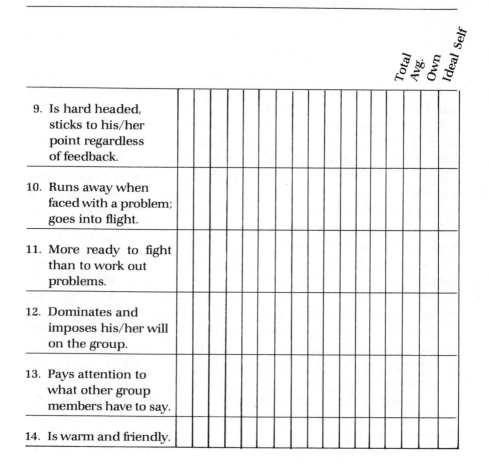

																						Total	Avg.	Own	Ideal Self
9. Is hard headed, sticks to his/her point regardless of feedback.																									
10. Runs away when faced with a problem; goes into flight.																									
11. More ready to fight than to work out problems.																									
12. Dominates and imposes his/her will on the group.																									
13. Pays attention to what other group members have to say.																									
14. Is warm and friendly.																									

Rating Scale: 7 = Always; 6 = Almost always; 5 = Fairly often; 4 = Sometimes; 3 = Not too often; 2 = Almost never; 1 = Never.

In actual use, the first factor analysis of the GME (using sixteen items, nine-point scales) revealed two factors: (A) group-oriented activity and (B) personal alienation (Snyder, 1970). The positive side of factor A includes assertive group participation, helpful involvement with others, and leadership. The less clearly delineated negative pole is characterized by withdrawal and avoidance of handling problems in the group. Factor A appears to describe task and maintenance behaviors. The positive role of factor B is heavily loaded with such items as "ready to fight," "annoys others," and "is hard headed." Other items of moderate loading are "dominates," "flight from problems," and "sets self apart." There is a moderately negative loading on "pays attention to what others say." Factor B appears to be related to individually oriented behaviors. A test-retest correlation from week one to week four (N = 64) was .633 and .568 for factors A and B, respectively.

Later studies (Baker et al., 1972) of the GME (using sixteen items, nine-point scales) yield additional data on reliability and factorial validity. The sixteen individual items were evaluated for interjudge reliability (using group members as judges) using Kendall's W on ten groups of ten men each for the sixth and sixteenth group sessions. The range of *W*s for the sixth session was from .28 to .61 and for the sixteenth session was .29 to .69. A W of .20 is needed for the 5 percent level of confidence.

A second factor analysis of the sixteen GME items on 217 subjects for mean-other, self, and ideal scores yielded eleven factors; three mean-other, four self, and four ideal factors. These factors were interpreted as:

Mean-Other	*Self*	*Ideal*
I: Alienation	IV: Alienation	VIII: Alienation
II: Task-Maintenance	V: Task-Maintenance	IX: Task-Maintenance
III: Talk	VI: Talk	X: Talk
	VII: Responsive to Group	XI: Responsive to Group

It will be noted that factors I and II in the Baker study correspond to factors B and A, respectively, in the Snyder study. All factors (I, II, B, and A) are based on mean-other ratings. The talk factor (III) relates to the two items used in the studies cited but not found on the forms in this book. These two items are: "talks about psychological problems" and "talks about medical problems." In summary, the two factor analyses completed on the GME appear to be consistent in revealing two factors on the mean-other ratings; Alienation (I and B) and Task-Maintenance (II and A). As indicated previously, a high item-by-item reliability also was found.

The Group Behavior Questionnaire

The Group Behavior Questionnaire (GBQ) is a twenty-three-item sociometric instrument that asks group members to choose two group members for each of the twenty-three items. Members are instructed to base their choices on the extent to which two other group members most resemble the descriptions of the items; i.e., members who take major responsibility for—or are identified with roles involving—leadership, communication, conflict, and dependency. This instrument helps group members to see how their own behavior is understood and valued by others as the group does it work. Items may be added or subtracted, depending on the goals of the group and the issues that the trainers want to identify.

The GBQ can be administered after the group has met for several days. Like the GME, the GBQ is more meaningful when the group members have had sufficient time to get to know each other well enough to make the ratings. Group members can post the numbers assigned to each individual on the roster and the data can be used to develop a group sociogram for each item and, if desired, for different time periods. The visual display of the data gives the group a picture of itself and has greater impact than would mere numbers. Sociograms can then be compared across groups to see what patterns of interaction emerge.

In the sample sociograms (Figure 2), it can be seen that on item 2, group members three and seven were chosen by most other members as having low influence during the first week. By the end of the second week, group member three becomes more influential, member six loses influence, and member seven stays the same. On item 4, members two and eight are most highly accepted by the group, with member eight receiving the largest number of choices. During the second week, group member five emerges, while member two loses ground. Member eight remains high in terms of acceptance. In looking at both the items used in this example, it becomes obvious that acceptance is not related to low influence. Members five and eight were most people's choices of high influence (item 1), which suggests that when group members are highly accepted, they also are given the power to influence the group.

The GBQ has been factor analyzed and appears to reflect the *status* of group members as opposed to *what* members *do* (as was true of the GME). Using these items, group members can be assigned factor scores on prominence, conflict proneness, and hyperdependency.

2. Which two are least able to influence others to change their opinions?

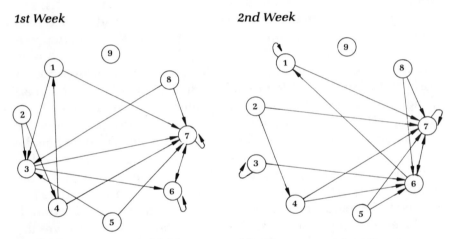

4. Which two are most highly accepted by the group at large?

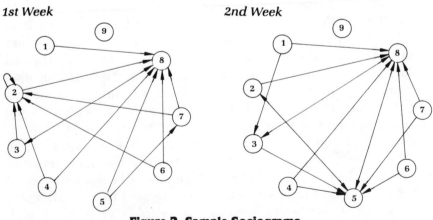

Figure 2. Sample Sociograms

The earliest factor analysis of the GBQ (Snyder, 1970) used only the first eighteen items on the instrument. Snyder found three factors, which he called leadership (I), contravention (II), and social impotence (III). Snyder did not rotate for a fourth factor, which would have made the first three cleaner in terms of unexplained variance. He also found that these three factors maintained their stability over four separate administrations (Table 2).

Table 2. Test-Retest Correlations for the GBQ

Interval		GBQ Factor		
	N	I	II	III
Weeks 1 & 2	91	.81	.76	.86
2 & 3	61	.81	.73	.84
3 & 4	47	.82	.79	.83
Weeks 1 & 3	61	.71	.65	.84
2 & 4	64	.83	.78	.85
Weeks 1 & 4	72	.75	.56	.82

Later factor analyses were conducted by Baker et al. (1972) and Baker (1973) using the twenty-three-item questionnaire completed by 217 respondents. Baker rotated the three, four, and five factors and, on the basis of a staff decision, settled for four factors. These factors were labeled leadership (I), conflict proneness (II), hyperdependency (III), and talk (IV). As can be seen, Baker's first three factors correspond to the three identified by Snyder. The four factors in the Baker study appear in Table 3, with some of their item loadings. Trainers can substitute items that are relevant to the issues they want to examine or use fewer items as desired. As with the GME and the GAS, when items are substituted on the GBQ, the original factors no longer hold true. This does not pose a problem for trainers, however, unless they are using the instrument for research purposes.

Table 3. Baker's Four Factors for the GBQ

I. Leadership	13	Which two seem to be the genuine leaders?
	1	Which two members of the group *can most easily* influence others to change their opinions?
	18	Which two have tried to do the most to keep the group "on the ball"?
	7	Which two *require the least help* in keeping up with group and laboratory activities?
II. Conflict Proneness	15	Which two have shown the most hostility in group meetings?
	3	Which two have clashed most sharply in the course of the group meetings?
	23	Which two say or do funny, sarcastic things that disrupt the group and hurt other members?
III. Hyperdependency	6	Which two *depend most on* the group members or staff in keeping up with group and laboratory activities?
	2	Which two *are least able* to influence others to change their opinions?
	5	Which two give in most easily to what other group members want?
	22	Which two show the least interest in getting the group moving?
IV. Talk	9	Which two are most likely to talk about their medical and physical problems?
	10	Which two are most likely to talk about their problems in dealing with others?

GROUP BEHAVIOR QUESTIONNAIRE

End of Week   1   2   3   4   Name _____

Data # _____   Date _____

Answer all questions by choosing members from your group who demonstrated the characteristics listed in the interactions that occurred in the group. Use the group members' group numbers in filling out this form. Choose two people in answer to each question. You may choose yourself. When you are not sure of your answer, make a guess, but please answer every question.

PART I

1. Which members of the group *can most easily* influence others to change their opinions?   _____   _____

2. Which two *are least able* to influence others to change their opinions?   _____   _____

3. Which two have clashed most sharply in the course of the group meetings?   _____   _____

4. Which two are most highly accepted by the group at large?   _____   _____

5. Which two give in most easily to what other group members want?   _____   _____

6. Which two *depend most on* the group members or staff in keeping up with group and laboratory activities?   _____   _____

7. Which two *require the least help* in keeping up with group and lab activities?   _____   _____

8. Which two try most to get attention from other group members?   _____   _____

9. Which two are most likely to talk about their medical and physcial problems?   _____   _____

10. Which two are most likely to talk about their problems in dealing with others?   _____   _____

11. Which two have shown the greatest desire to accomplish something?   _____   _____

12. Which two have been most ready to discuss topics not directly related to the group's task?   _____   _____

13. Which two seem to be the genuine leaders?   _____   _____

14. Which two have shown the strongest need for direction and support?   _____   _____

15. Which two have shown the most hostility in group meetings?   _____   _____

16. Which two have wanted the group to be warm, friendly, and comfortable?   _____   _____

17. Which two have competed the most with others, in the sense of rivalry?   _____   _____

18. Which two have tried to do the most to keep the group "on the ball"?   _____   _____

19. Which two do *you* usually *talk to* the most?   _____   _____

20. Which two do *you* usually *talk to* the least?   _____   _____

When there is a lot of tension and nervousness in the group and everybody seems to be wrapped up in his or her own problems, which two group members do each of the following:

21. Say or do funny things that relax members and get the group working again?   _____   _____

22. Show the least interest in getting the group moving?   _____   _____

23. Say or do funny, sarcastic things that disrupt the group and hurt other members?   _____   _____

PART II

Now, taking the training as a whole, to which three people do you usually talk the most?

_____

_____

_____

The Participation Scale

Undoubtedly, the most important dimension of group activity is participation. This dimension is important not only as a fairly reliable measure of personality but also is useful in increasing the group members' awareness of a singularly universal and crucial aspect of behavior—how much they talk. Participation is not a unidimensional aspect of behavior but is extremely complex and is related to a wide variety of other behaviors. In studies at the VA's Human Interaction Training Laboratory (Baker et al., 1972), it was found that participation in small, self-directed groups was significantly related to the following items as rated by other group members (mean-other ratings).

Table 4. Correlates of Participation ($\bar{X}$ others)*

(N = 109)

$\underline{r}$	Variable**
.78	Self-rating on participation
.78	Takes lead in selecting topics and procedures, GME
.74	Competes with others—rivalry, GBQ
.67	Can most easily influence others, GBQ
.67	Tries most to get attention from others, GBQ
.66	Helps members express their ideas and feelings, GME
.66	Dominates and imposes will on group, GME
.64	Seems to be genuine leader, GBQ
.62	Requires least help with lab and group activities, GBQ
.62	Expresses himself clearly, GME
.60	Talked to the most, GBQ
.60	Provides helpful feedback to others, GME
.59	Prominence, GME
.59	Conflict proneness, GME

-.59	Gives in most easily to what others want, GBQ
.57	Clashes most sharply in course of meetings, GBQ
.56	Helps group stay on target, GME
.53	Keeps group "on the ball," GBQ
.52	Talks about problems in dealing with others, GBQ
-.51	Least able to influence others, GBQ
.50	Talks about medical problems, GBQ
.46	Most highly accepted by group, GBQ
-.44	Talked to the least, GBQ
.43	Hard headed—sticks to point regardless of feedback, GME
-.43	Depends most on group or staff for keeping up, GBQ
-.41	Strongest need for direction and support, GBQ
.41	Levels with other members, GME
.30	Dominance, CPI
.27	Self-acceptance (Sa), CPI
.26	Capacity for status (Cs), CPI
.26	Social presence, MMPI
.25	Sociability (sy), CPI
.25	IQ, AGCT
.24	Intellectual efficiency (Ie), CPI

*   r of .190 = .05; r of .248 = .01

** GME: Group Member Evaluation
  GBQ: Group Behavior Questionnaire (Sociometric)
  CPI: California Personality Inventory
AGCT: Army General Classification Test (Intelligence)
MMPI: Minnesota Multiphasic Personality Inventory

Participation reliability and interjudge reliability (to provide an external criterion of participation to evaluate the validity of the participants' ratings) also were established. In addition, each group member rated every other member on participation and was assigned a participation score that was the mean of others' ratings of him (mean-other score). The mean-other participation score correlated .88 with the amount of talking determined by external judges. These studies demonstrate that participation can be rated reliably by judges and that group members' ratings of each others' participation is a valid measure of the amount of talking they do in the group sessions.

As can be seen, people who are active in groups tend to elicit a wider variety of reactions from other group members than do less active members. High participators expose more facets of themselves and provide more behavioral data to which group members can respond.

The Participation Scale can be used after each group session or periodically. Group members are rated by their numbers on the group's roster. The person doing the rating finds his or her own group number along the top of the graph and rates the other group members (the numbers in the left margin) in the column of boxes under the rater's number. Each participant rates every participant, including himself or herself, on the amount the person talked in the group session. A daily participation score is assigned to each individual, based on an average of all group members' ratings (self-ratings excluded) to produce a mean-other score. Weekly participation scores or a final participation score can be computed from the daily mean-other scores for all the sessions of the program. Mean-other ratings can be ranked to determine high, medium, and low participation. In this way, each individual's level of participation can be tracked over the course of the workshop, and the individual's self-ratings can be compared with the group's ratings of that person. These records of participation can then provide the basis for structured interventions designed to create a more equal distribution of participation.

PARTICIPATION SCALE

Date ____________________ Name ____________________

Instructions: Rate each member of your group on participation in *this* meeting according to the following 9-point scale:

9 Talked constantly
8 Talked almost all of the time
7 Talked most of the time
6 Talked a lot
5 Talked a moderate amount
4 Talked some
3 Talked a little
2 Talked very little
1 Did not talk at all

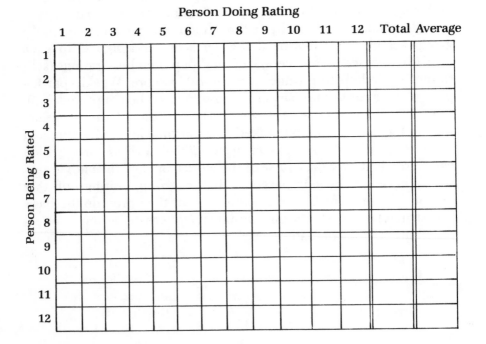

Person Doing Rating

Person Being Rated	1	2	3	4	5	6	7	8	9	10	11	12	Total	Average
1														
2														
3														
4														
5														
6														
7														
8														
9														
10														
11														
12														

Participation interaction charts also can be used by observers to record the amount and direction of interpersonal interactions. Figure 3 illustrates a completed chart with explanations.

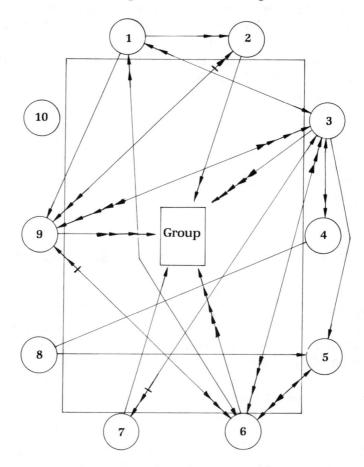

Note: Arrows indicate direction of communication. Number of arrowheads indicate number of times one member talked to another member. Arrows and arrowheads to "group" indicate times an individual looked at two or more group members when he or she talked. Cross lines indicate an interruption or when one member cut off another member.

Figure 3. Sample Participation Interaction Chart

As has been shown in the preceding discussion, instruments can be used regularly to aid in processing individual group sessions, as a means of tracking particular processes over several sessions, or to evaluate a total workshop. With groups that typically do not use them, instruments can still be introduced profitably to obtain quick and relatively objective readings on particular group sessions. It is important in using instruments to select items that are (a) relevant to issues with which the group is struggling but that are not yet apparent; (b) sensitive to individual patterns of participation; (c) useful for diagnosing the current status of the group; (d) important in assessing the group's reaction to a particular activity, intervention, or meeting; and (e) relevant to individual, group, and workshop goals. The trainer and group members should decide what dimensions they would like to assess and then select or develop items that reflect those issue.

AN INTRODUCTION TO STRUCTURED ACTIVITIES

There are events and processes that emerge naturally at some time during the life of most groups. When the group is unstructured, the trainer may alert the group to the event and in some way facilitate the members' dealing with, and learning from, the event. Another way to handle group events is to diagnose the issue and to provide a structured experience to help the members examine and work through the issue. Structured experiences also can be used to enrich a particular event by exposing more facets of that event than would ordinarily be available to the group members. The structured experiences described in this chapter represent only a sample of the ways in which important concepts and events can be used to facilitate the participants' learning. They are not the only way to explore these events, nor should they be used without consideration of their relevance to what is happening or will happen in the group (see Pfeiffer & Jones, 1980).

Structured *experiences,* in which the dynamics of and learnings from the activity are processed, should not be confused with structured *exercises,* in which the intent is not to generate new data or learnings, but merely to illustrate a technique or practice a skill. These latter activities also can be valuable learning tools. Structured exercises generally take less time to complete and to process and they require less skill on the part of the trainer. Both types of structured activities are presented in this book. They vary in format and in content. Most of them are accompanied (after the procedural instructions) by the work sheets that are needed and/or by theory handouts to acquaint the participants with what will occur or to aid them in processing what has occurred. Each activity is cross-referenced so that the reader can refer to the textual discussion of the subject matter.

The Use of Theory Handouts

In human relations training workshops, conceptual learning is obtained in several ways: one is through the presentation of theory by the training staff; another is the abstraction of theory from ongoing experiences (a joint effort of both participants and staff); a third way is through handouts of previously prepared materials; and the final method is the combination of any or all three of the preceding methods. The most effective learning results from the combination of all three, i.e., the trainer presents a background lecturette, the participants engage in an activity in which they actually experience the dynamics or effects that have been discussed, and, finally, the participants are provided with a theory handout that they can read and reflect on as they integrate their learnings.

If the group members know that they will receive a theory handout, they are relieved of the need to take notes and can concentrate more fully on what is being said or done. In addition, the handouts provide the participants with a record of the learnings from the workshop, which can be used to promote continued learning after the participants have returned home.

ACTIVITIES FOR IMPLEMENTING
AND PRACTICING FEEDBACK

CHECK LIST FOR GIVING FEEDBACK

Objectives

1. To develop the participants' awareness of their own styles of giving feedback and the effect of these styles on the receptiveness of the receivers.
2. To enable the participants to modify the ways in which they give feedback and to observe the consequences of these changes.
3. To help the participants to practice giving and receiving feedback more spontaneously over the course of the workshop and to enable them to monitor their practice.

Instructions for Group Members

Following are some rating scales that describe different ways of giving feedback. Take a few minutes to think about your own feedback style in your present group. To what extent do you use or not use the methods suggested? Go through the items on the check list, one by one, and draw a circle around the number on each scale that best characterizes your feedback style. Try to think of concrete examples (that have occurred in the group) for each item.

When all members have completed the seven items, share your ratings with the group. Solicit feedback from other group members about how they see your feedback style and compare these impressions with how you rated yourself. Obtain reactions and examples from as many group members as you can. Listen carefully and ask for clarification if you do not understand something. Do not try to explain or defend your position. You may want to ask the other group members to indicate how they would have rated you on each item. In this way you can keep a tally of their ratings along with your self-ratings. On the basis of your own ratings and the feedback you receive from other group members, check those items on which you want to work and on which you want continuing feedback from the group.

Giving feedback effectively is a skill that can be developed through your interactions with other group members and your openness to being influenced by them. It should be stressed, however, that a critical dimension in developing feedback skills is your own attitude toward yourself and others in terms of being nonjudgmental and more accepting.

Check List for Giving Feedback[3]

Least Effective Method		Rating				Most Effective Method
1. *Indirect Expression of Feeling.* Not describing your own emotional state, e.g., "You are a very likeable person."	1	2	3	4	5	*Direct Expression of Feeling.* "Owning your own feelings by describing your emotional state, e.g., "I like you very much."
2. *Attributive Feedback.* Ascribing motives to behavior, e.g., "You are angry with me."	1	2	3	4	5	*Descriptive Feedback.* Observing and describing the behavior to which you are reacting, e.g., "You are frowning and your hands are clenched in a fist."
3. *Evaluative Feedback.* Passing judgment on another person's behavior or imposing "standards," e.g., "You *shouldn't* be so angry."	1	2	3	4	5	*Nonevaluative Feedback.* Commenting on behavior without judging its worth or value, e.g., "Your anger is as legitimate a feeling as any other."
4. *General Feedback.* Stating broad reactions and not indicating specific behaviors, e.g., "You're pretty touchy today."	1	2	3	4	5	*Specific Feedback.* Pointing out the specific actions to which you are reacting, e.g., "When you frowned, I felt anxious."

[3]Reprinted from Philip G. Hanson, "Giving Feedback: An Interpersonal Skill." In John E. Jones and J. William Pfeiffer (Eds.), *The 1975 Annual Handbook for Group Facilitators.* San Diego, CA: University Associates, 1975.

5. *Pressure to Change.*   1   2   3   4   5   *Freedom of Choice to*
Implying that people   *Change.* Allowing others
are not behaving ac-   to decide whether they
cording to your stan-   want to change their be-
dards, e.g., "Don't call   havior, e.g., "When you
me 'Sonny'!"   called me 'Sonny,' I felt
                                              put down."

6. *Delayed Feedback.*   1   2   3   4   5   *Immediate Feedback.*
Postponing feedback   Responding immediately
to others' behavior until   after the event, e.g., "I'm
later, e.g., "I was really   feeling hurt because
hurt yesterday when you   you're not responding to
ignored me."   me."

7. *External Feedback.*   1   2   3   4   5   *Group-Shared Feedback.*
Focusing attention on   Focusing attention on
events *outside* the   events that occur *in* the
group, e.g., "My friends   group, e.g., "Does this
see me as being very   group see me as being
supportive."   very supportive?"

The JoHari Window: Self-Rating—Subgroup Sharing

Objectives

1. To describe open and closed behavior in terms of the JoHari Window model.
2. To identify facilitating and inhibiting forces that affect the exchange of feedback.
3. To encourage the increase of open behavior in the group through practice in the exchange of feedback.

Time

Approximately two and one-half hours.

Instructions for the Trainer

   1. Begin by giving a lecturette to the total group on giving and receiving feedback, using the JoHari Window model (Chapter Three, pages 61-69). (You may furnish handouts of the JoHari Window model or illustrate it yourself on newsprint.) Central to the lecturette, emphasize how decreasing the "Blind Spot," the area unknown to self, and decreasing the "Facade," the area unknown to others, will increase the "Arena," the area known to everyone, thereby fostering openness. Also emphasize the role of meaningful feedback in this process.

2. Distribute the JoHari Window Self-Rating Sheets and pencils.

3. Suggest that one goal that participants in a group setting may have is to discover data about themselves that they were previously unaware of, i.e., to decrease their Blind Spots. Stress that the only way they may do this is through the process of receiving feedback, which means that they must actively solicit feedback and be receptive to it when they receive it. In terms of the JoHari Window model, the vertical line will move to the right as the Blind Spot is decreased.

4. Illustrate the decreasing Blind Spot on newsprint using the following model:

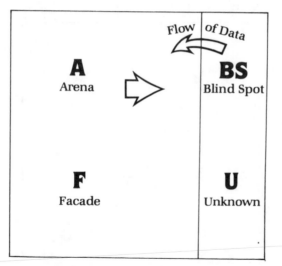

(This and all other newsprint illustrations should be posted at the front of the room with masking tape for later reference.)

5. Ask the participants to look at their Self-Rating Sheets. Point out that a scale from one to nine, describing the extent to which a person solicits feedback, runs across the top of the sheet. Ask the members of the group to think back to their last group meeting(s) and of the times during that meeting when they felt curious about

how they were being perceived by others, i.e., how many times they wanted to know how other group members were feeling about them and how they were "coming across" to the group.

6. Direct the members to look at the scale across the top of the blank window again and to find a location on that scale that describes the extent to which they *actually solicited* feedback in that group session. Emphasize that they are not to rate how many times they *felt* the need for feedback or how many times they received it without asking for it, but how many times they *actually asked* for it. Tell them to draw a vertical line to the bottom of the window from the point that they have located on the top scale. (Illustrate this on the posted model.)

7. Now suggest that another goal that members may have in the group setting is to become more open or visible to the group by disclosing some of the personal reactions and feelings that they have kept to themselves or by giving feedback to others, i.e., decreasing the Facade. Illustrate how the horizontal line drops when the Facade is decreased:

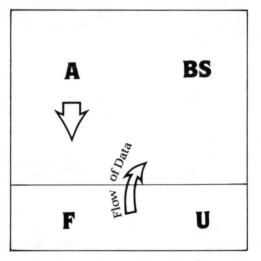

8. Tell the group to notice how the Arena increases as the Blind Spot and Facade decrease. Ask the members to look at their JoHari Window Self-Rating Sheets again to notice on the left margin a scale running from one to nine—measuring the extent to which a person discloses himself or herself or gives feedback to the group. Direct the members to think back to their last group

meeting(s) and to remember how many times during that group session they felt the need to (a) give feedback to other group members, (b) express their own feelings and perceptions about themselves, or (c) take a stand on group issues.

9. Now tell them to locate on the left margin of the scale the position that indicates the extent to which they *actually gave* feedback *or disclosed* themselves to the group. Emphasize that they are to rate only the extent to which they actually gave feedback, not how many times they felt like doing so. When all members have located their positions on the scale, direct them to draw a horizontal line across the window pane (Illustrate this on a new model and post it.)

10. At this point, illustrate the use of the JoHari Window model by interpreting variously constructed windows. (Illustrations of the Open window, the Interviewer, the Bull in the China Shop, and the Turtle are described in Chapter Three, pages 67-69.)

11. When the interpretive part of the lecturette is completed, divide the group into triads or quartets.

12. Ask the participants to take twenty-to-thirty minutes to share their windows within their subgroups. Tell them to ask the members of their subgroups for feedback on how they would have rated the individuals in terms of soliciting and giving feedback and then to compare their self-ratings with the perceptions of the other members. When this exchange is completed, direct the members to begin to identify the forces in their groups that make it easy or difficult to solicit or give feedback and then, as a subgroup, to make a list of the facilitating and inhibiting forces. Tell them that they will have about fifteen minutes to accomplish this task and supply newsprint and felt-tipped markers to each subgroup.

13. When the groups have completed their lists, convene the participants and ask them to share the information generated in the subgroups. Have them integrate the subgroup lists into a final list of forces and discuss what steps the group wants to take in order to increase the facilitating forces and decrease the inhibiting forces in the feedback process. Participants may be encouraged to make contracts with one another to exchange feedback in the future.

JoHari Window Self-Rating Sheet[4]

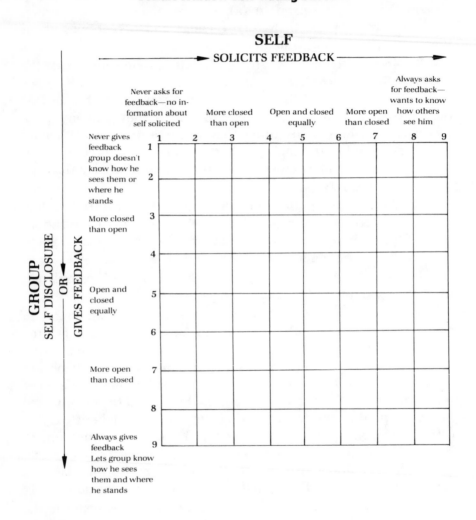

SELF

SOLICITS FEEDBACK →

[4]Reprinted from Philip G. Hanson, "Analyzing and Increasing Open Behavior: The JoHari Window." In John E. Jones and J. William Pfeiffer (Eds.), *The 1973 Annual Handbook for Group Facilitators*. San Diego, CA: University Associates, 1973.

STRUCTURED EXPERIENCE: GROUP OBSERVATIONS

Objectives

1. To develop an awareness of *how* groups work and sensitivity to the dimensions of group behavior that facilitate or block effective team work.
2. To provide participants with an opportunity to practice giving and receiving feedback on a group level.
3. To prepare participants to assume a participant-observer orientation within their own groups.
4. To assist groups in evaluating different ways in which ongoing group issues are handled.
5. To prepare the groups for later work in observing and designing interventions for another group.
6. To expand internal group cohesion, which usually results when groups feel that they are being "evaluated" by others.

Time

Two and one-half hours.

Instructions

1. Groups are paired off; one group in each pair is designated as group A and the other group is designated as group B. The Scott General Hospital Problem Sheet is distributed to all members, and the members of all "A" groups receive a copy of Problem A, while the members of all "B" groups receive a copy of Problem B.

2. Groups are directed to rank the solutions to the problem assigned to them from the best choice (1) to the worst choice (5). (Ten to fifteen minutes.)

3. The observation guide, What To Look for in Groups, is distributed, and the trainer gives a lecturette covering the group dimensions and giving examples.

4. After the lecturette, group members count off and each member in a group is assigned a different topic from the observation guide; for example, the number ones in each group take "participation," the number twos take "influence," and so on. "Styles of Influence," the last section in the observation guide represents a summary of many of the other dimensions clustered into four categories and is not assigned as an observation item. Each pair of groups is seated in a "fishbowl" arrangement, with the B group seated in a circle in the center and the A group seated around it on the outside. The participants are told that the paired groups will take turns observing each other and providing feedback. (Each pair of groups can be assigned to a separate room, if this much space is available.)

5. The trainer posts the observation schedule on newsprint.

Group Observation Schedule

Twenty minutes: group A observes group B
Ten minutes: group A gives feedback to group B
Five minutes: group B responds to group A

Then

Twenty minutes: group B observes group A
Ten minutes: group B gives feedback to group A
Five minutes: group A responds to group B

The trainer tells each A (working) group that its task is to reach group agreement on its members' individual rankings of the problem solutions from the Scott Hospital case. The groups begin working.

6. At the end of twenty minutes the discussions are stopped, whether or not group agreement has been reached. The members of each observing group present their observations to the members of the group that they observed, with each observer stating what process area he or she was observing. During this time the members of the working group do not respond, but can take notes.

7. After the feedback is completed, the working group is directed to respond and ask for clarification. At this time defensive reactions frequently surface, and it is important to emphasize that, for whatever reasons, for twenty minutes of interaction the observing group saw what it saw. The group that was observed can be advised that rather than rejecting the feedback, it would be more useful if it would accept it, examine it in terms of the group's history, and then reject it or remain alert to the possibility of that behavior occurring the future.

8. The groups are reversed and the procedure is repeated. (If the schedule allows, a coffee break can be announced before the process begins again.)

Scott General Hospital Problem Sheet

Scott General Hospital is a moderately sized, municipally-run, general hospital in a city of 1,200,000 persons, located on the East Coast. The staff of the hospital comprises 1,500 persons. The position of chief nurse, recently vacated, has just been filled by Mrs. Farron.

The hospital hired Mrs. Farron from a professional employment agency, which recommended her for being diligent, hard working, efficient, and progressive. Indeed, the hospital was searching for such qualities. Mrs. Farron had attended several human relations training and management development workshops and had developed a management philosophy consistent with her training.

The chief nurse who had just retired had allowed the wards to run on a haphazard, catch-as-catch-can basis. The work load of the nursing staff had been unevenly distributed; there were no work assignments, and it was not uncommon for the nursing staff to have a lot of absenteeism. Often, there was no additional help in the wards during these absences. Mrs. Farron knew that this type of laissez-faire management produced frustration and low morale in a working force. When she was hired, it was made clear that it would be her responsibility to iron out these difficulties. She spent her first week in the hospital as an observer, making the rounds and acquainting herself with the situation.

There was no doubt in Mrs. Farron's mind that, in addition to the work problems already noted, the morale of the staff was very low. The question she asked herself was "How can I deal *most effectively* with the problem of getting more work accomplished and at the same time increase staff morale?" She had some understanding of the intimate but complex relationship between how well people do their jobs and their feelings of satisfaction with themselves and with their work associates and she knew that happy people tend to produce more work. She knew that there were several strategies she could adopt and that not all of them would be equally effective. Mrs. Farron had to decide on a strategy by the time of the next weekly staff meeting.

Your Group's Task

Rank from one to five, in order of effectiveness, the five possible strategies available to Mrs. Farron. A rank of number one indicates the best solution to the problem; number two, the second best, and so on.

Problem A

The decision-making process at Scott Hospital's nursing-staff meetings was completely ineffective. Two or three people carried the conversation most of the time and were primarily responsible for most of the decisions made. These decisions, however, were seldom carried out because of lack of support from the other staff members. Mrs. Farron decided to:

_____ a.   Go along with what others in the group decide but without much apparent involvement or pushing, so that her subordinates will be involved and not overly influenced by her. She will let others make the decisions, explaining that "it's their show."

_____ b.   Try to help the group achieve a compromise between its goal and group morale. When there are several possible decisions the group can make, she will call for democratic voting procedures. This results in reasonable action and satisfies the majority of people concerned.

_____ c.   Make decisions and start actions as she sees best. When she "sets" her mind on a good idea, she will plow through with it. In group meetings, she will push for hard-and-fast decisions for action because when it takes too much time to work out decisions and plans, the staff gets bogged down.

_____ d.   Aim for decisions based on the full planning and cooperation of all concerned, preferring meetings in which the group's goals and objectives are planned first and then achieved through full participation. She is wary of decisions that are rushed through the group over objections and without opportunity for consideration of alternatives.

_____ e.   Quickly offer agreement and support to others' ideas because she knows how important friendly staff relations are and how crippling conflict can be. She will tend to postpone or avoid difficult decisions in order to reduce tension and keep the peace. She will try to have group meetings that are friendly and easygoing rather than aggressive, tough, work sessions.

Problem B

At the first nursing-staff meeting, the question of summer vacations came up. There was considerable resentment among the newer staff members about the long-term staff people having priority choice for the summer months. One member was particularly upset about this preferential treatment because he had been forced to take his vacations when his children were in school. Encouraged by him, other members began to express their resentment to Mrs. Farron. Feelings began to run high and voices became louder and louder. Mrs. Farron decided to:

_____ a. Get into the thick of it and state her own opinions clearly and firmly. Since she is in charge of the group, she will handle conflict by "putting the lid on it," saying,"Let's get back to the facts and leave feelings out of this discussion."

_____ b. Try to get to the core of the problem. She wants those involved to learn how and why the problem developed in order to resolve it in such a manner that it will not recur in the future and the effectiveness of the individual staff members will not be diminished by this conflict.

_____ c. Avoid committing herself in situations involving conflict and tension because she does not want to prejudice the decisions of the staff. Her participation will be minimal; she will be noncommittal and show a "hands-off" attitude, encouraging the staff members to "sit down together and work it out."

_____ d. Try to arbitrate the conflict and achieve a compromise—to find moderately agreeable solutions and decisions that will not hurt the organization much and will be fairly acceptable to most of those concerned.

_____ e. Smooth over people's feelings and try to keep them from getting angry (without exploring the reasons behind the tensions). She wants to avoid conflict in the group at any cost, because she knows how destructive it can be to congenial and cooperative staff relations.

What To Look for in Groups[5]

There are two major ingredients in all human interactions: content and process. The first deals with subject matter, or the task on which the group is working. In most interactions, the focus of attention of all persons is on the content. The second ingredient, process, is what happens between and to group members while the group is working. Group process includes such items as morale, atmosphere, influence, participation, leadership struggles, conflict, competition, cooperation, etc. In most interactions, very little attention is paid to process, even when it is the major cause of ineffective group action. Sensitivity to group processes will better enable members to diagnose group problems early and deal with them more effectively. Since these processes are present in all groups, awareness of them will enhance a member's worth to a group and make that person a more effective participant.

Below are some observation guidelines to help in observing and analyzing group behavior.

Participation

One indication of involvement is verbal participation. Look for differences in the amount of participation among members.

1. Who are the high participators?
2. Who are the low participators?
3. Do you see any shift in participation, e.g., highs become quiet; lows suddenly become talkative? Do you see any possible reason for this in the group's interaction?
4. How are silent people treated? How is their silence interpreted? As consent? Disagreement? Disinterest? Fear?
5. Who talks to whom? Do you see any reason for this in the group's interactions?
6. Who keeps the ball rolling? Why? Do you see any reason for this in the group's interactions?

Influence

Influence and participation are not the same. Some people may speak very little, yet capture the attention of the whole group. Others may talk a lot but are generally not listened to by other members.

1. Which members are high in influence, i.e., when they talk others seem to listen to or follow them?

---

[5]Adapted from Philip G. Hanson, "What To Look for in Groups: An Observation Guide." In J. William Pfeiffer and John E. Jones (Eds.), *The 1972 Annual Handbook for Group Facilitators.* San Diego, CA: University Associates, 1972.

2. Which members are low in influence, i.e., others do not listen to or follow them?
3. Is there any shift in influence? Who shifts? How?
4. Do you see any rivalry in the group? Is there a struggle for leadership? What effect does this have on other group members?
5. What do members do that leads to high influence?

Decision-Making Procedures

Many kinds of decision are made in groups without consideration of the effects of those decisions on other members. Some people try to impose their own decisions on the group, while others want all members to participate or share in the decisions that are made.

1. Does anyone make a (self-authorized) decision and carry it out without checking with other group members? What effect does this have on other group members?
2. Does the group drift from topic to topic? Who topic-jumps? Do you see any reason for this in the group's interactions?
3. Who supports other members' suggestions or decisions? Does this support result in the two members deciding the topic or activity for the group? How does this "handclasp" procedure affect other group members?
4. Is there any evidence of a majority pushing a decision through over other members' objections? Do the majority members call for a vote?
5. Is there any attempt to get all members to participate in a consensus decision? What effect does this seem to have on the group?
6. Does anyone make contributions that do not receive any kind of response or recognition? What effect does this "plop" have on the member?

Task Functions

These functions illustrate behaviors that are concerned with getting the job done or accomplishing the task that the group has before it.

1. Does anyone ask for or make suggestions about the best way to proceed or tackle a problem?
2. Does anyone attempt to summarize what has been discussed or what has been going on in the group?
3. Does anyone ask for or give facts, ideas, opinions, feelings, feedback; does anyone search for alternatives?
4. Does anyone keep the group on target and prevent topic jumping or going off on tangents?
5. Does anyone amplify or build on contributions from others?

Maintenance Functions

These functions are important to the morale of the group. They maintain good and harmonious working relationships among the members and create a group atmosphere that enables each member to contribute the most. They insure smooth and effective teamwork within the group.

1. Who helps others enter the discussion (gate openers)?
2. Who cuts off others or interrupts them (gate closers)?
3. How well do members succeed in getting their ideas across? Do some members seem to be preoccupied or not listening? Are there any attempts by group members to help others clarify their ideas?
4. How are ideas rejected? How do members react when their ideas are not accepted? Do members attempt to support others when they reject their ideas?
5. Does anyone check for feelings in others?

Group Atmosphere

Something about the way in which a group works creates an observable atmosphere in the group. People may differ in the kind of atmosphere they like in a group. Insight can be gained into the characteristics of a group by observing the general group climate.

1. Who seems to prefer a friendly, congenial atmosphere? Is there any attempt to suppress conflict or unpleasant feelings?
2. Who seems to prefer an atmosphere of conflict and tension?
3. Do people seem involved and interested? Is the atmosphere one of reward, cooperation, competition, work, play, sluggishness, fighting, taking flight, or tension? Which seems most apparent?

Membership

A major concern for group members is the degree of acceptance or inclusion they feel in the group. Different patterns of interaction may develop in the group that gives clues about the degrees and kinds of membership.

1. Is there any subgrouping? Do two or three members consistently agree with and support one another or consistently disagree with or oppose one another?
2. Do some people seem to be "outside" the group? Do some members seem to be more "in?" How are the "outsiders" treated?
3. Do some members move in and out of the group? Under what conditions do they move in or out?

Feelings

During any group discussion, feelings are generated by the interactions between members. These feelings, however, are seldom discussed. Observers must guess about them based on the tones of voice, facial expressions, gestures, or other nonverbal cues given by members.

1. What signs of emotion do you observe in group members?
2. Do you see any attempts by group members to block the expression of feelings, particularly negative feelings? How is this done? Does anyone do this consistently?
3. Does anyone support or encourage the expression of feelings? How is this done? How is it received?

Norms

Standards or rules may develop in a group to control the behavior of its members. Norms usually express the beliefs or desires of the majority of the group members about what behaviors *should* or *should not* take place in the group. These norms may be clear to all members (explicit), be known or sensed by only a few (implicit), or operate completely below the level of awareness of all group members. Some norms help the group to progress and some hinder it.

1. Are certain topical areas avoided in the group? Who seems to reinforce this avoidance? How do they do it?
2. Are group members overly nice or polite to each other? Are only positive feelings expressed? Do members agree with each other too readily? What happens when members disagree?
3. Do you see norms operating about participation or the kinds of questions that are allowed, e.g., "If I tell my problems you have to tell your problems?" Do members feel free to question each other about their feelings? Do questions tend to be restricted to intellectual topics or events outside the group?

Styles of Influence

Influence can take many forms. It can be positive or negative; it can enlist the support or cooperation of others or alienate them. *How* a person attempts to influence another may be the crucial factor in determining how open or closed the other will be toward being influenced. Four styles of influence frequently emerge in groups.

1. *Autocratic:* Does anyone attempt to impose his will or values on other group members or try to coerce them into supporting his decisions? Does anyone evaluate or pass judgment on other group members? Do any members block action when it is not moving in the direction they desire? Does anyone push to "get the group organized"?
2. *Peacemaker:* Does anyone eagerly support other group members' decisions? Does anyone consistently try to avoid the expression of conflict or unpleasant feelings by "pouring oil on the troubled waters"? Is any member typically deferential toward other group members—giving them power? Do any members appear to avoid giving negative feedback?

3. *Laissez Faire:* Do any group members attract attention by their apparent lack of involvement in the group? Does any group member go along with group decisions without seeming to commit himself one way or the other? Does anyone seem to be withdrawn and uninvolved, not initiate activity, or participate mechanically and only in response to other members' questions?
4. *Democratic:* Does anyone try to include everyone in a group decision or discussion? Does anyone express his feelings and opinions openly and directly without evaluating or judging others? Does this person encourage others to do the same? Do any members appear to be open to feedback and criticism from others? When feelings run high and tension mounts, do some members attempt to deal with the conflict in a problem-solving way?

Role Playing: A Type of Structured Experience

A classic structural intervention in training is role playing.[6] This technique works so well that it is often either the first choice of the trainer or the last desperate choice! With large groups, role playing in dyads or triads usually works very well because it involves *all* participants. In a larger workshop (forty participants or more), one needs an effective mechanism with which to track all the data that are generated from numerous simultaneous role plays. One tracking mechanism is the shifting-observer role. The tracking of role plays is provided by individual observer ratings for each interaction. These ratings are collected, summarized, and posted for examination and discussion by all participants.

Rather than involving all participants in active roles and devising a tracking mechanism, the beginning trainer frequently is tempted to designate several participants to be actors in a group role play and use the rest of the participants as observers. This design is basically a play and it rarely works except as a play. The theatrical setting encourages overacting and competition so that it is difficult to maintain the simulation or effect of a real situation.

---

[6]Group role playing should not be confused with *psychodrama*, which incorporates special techniques, utilizes a director, and is directed toward the growth of one principal (or protagonist).

Role playing as a legitimate learning mechanism provides the participants with an opportunity to experience, "try on," and/or practice new behaviors in an environment that is relatively free of threat. Role playing is used widely in leadership and management development to practice listening, problem-solving, and appraisal skills; in personal-effectiveness training to practice listening, communication, and risk-taking skills; and in team development to practice communication, information-sharing, and problem-solving skills, among others. A role play can be brief or very complex; it can highlight one issue or many related issues. Group members can exchange roles in order to experience all sides of a situation. They also can practice being "in the other person's shoes," and can provide feedback to one another on their styles of interacting. Finally, role playing can be used to work through issues or problems that arise in real life but which are difficult to examine objectively as they occur (Jones & Pfeiffer, 1979; Maier, Solem, & Maier, 1975; Shaw, Corsini, Blake, and Mouton, 1980).

It is important that the trainer emphasize the serious but experimental nature of a role play, lest participants treat it merely as fun or as an opportunity to "dump" pent-up emotions on others. The trainer also must allow sufficient time at the end of a role play for participants to "de-role" and to process their reaction to the experience and what they learned from it.

REFERENCES

Baker, R.R. *An empirical comparison of factor matching indices.* Unpublished manuscript, Human Interaction Training Laboratory, Veterans Administration Medical Center, Houston, TX, 1971. (Also in Catalog of Selected Documents in Psychology, 1973, 3, 116)

Baker, R., Hanson, P.G., & O'Connell, W.E. *Instrumentation studies.* Human Interaction Training Laboratory, Veterans Administration Medical Center, Unpublished manuscript, 1972. (Available from Philip G. Hanson, Veterans Administration Hospital, 2002 Holcombe Blvd., Houston, TX 77211)

Bales, R.F. *Personality and interpersonal behavior.* New York: Holt, Rinehart and Winston, 1970.

Blake, R.R., & Mouton, J.S. *The managerial grid*. Houston, TX: Gulf, 1964.

Burke, R., & Hanson, P.G. *Dimensions of group leadership*. Training and Measurement Systems. Houston, TX: 1976. (Instrument)

Gibb, J.R. TORI group self-diagnosis scale. In J.E. Jones & J.W. Pfeiffer (Eds.), *The 1977 annual handbook for group facilitators*. San Diego, CA: University Associates, 1977.

Jones, J.E., & Pfeiffer, J.W. Role playing. In J.E. Jones & J.W. Pfeiffer (Eds.), *The 1979 annual handbook for group facilitators*. San Diego, CA: University Associates, 1979.

Lake, D.G., Miles, M.B., & Earle, R.B., Jr. *Measuring human behavior*. New York: Teachers College Press, 1973.

Leary, T. *Interpersonal diagnoses of personality*. New York: Ronald Press, 1957.

Maier, N.R.F., Solem, A.R., & Maier, A.A. *The role-play technique: A handbook for management and leadership practice*. San Diego, CA: University Associates, 1975.

Pfeiffer, J.W., Heslin, R., & Jones, J.E. *Instrumentation in human relations training*. San Diego, CA: University Associates, 1976.

Pfeiffer, J.W., & Jones, J.E. Introduction to the structured experiences section. In J.W. Pfeiffer & J.E. Jones (Eds.), *The 1980 annual handbook for group facilitators*. San Diego, CA: University Associates, 1980.

Schutz, W. *FIRO awareness scales manual*. Palo Alto, CA: Consulting Psychologists Press, 1978.

Shaw, M.E., Corsini, R.J., Blake, R.R., & Mouton, J.S. *Role playing: A practical manual for group facilitators*. San Diego, CA: University Associates, 1980.

Snyder, R. *A study of behavior interactions in autonomous groups*. Unpublished doctoral dissertation, University of Houston, 1970.

Chapter 6
Guidelines for the Trainer

TRAINER ETHICS AND RESPONSIBILITY

A trainer who accepts a staff role in a training workshop assumes responsibility for his or her own behavior and its consequences. Trainers bring to the workshop their own sets of personal and professional values and needs, which should be made explicit whenever appropriate. Because of the trainers' roles and the power invested in them, the possibilities for manipulation, personal gain, and acting out of personal needs always are present. In addition, the need to be seen as competent can severely restrict the flexibility of a trainer. If this need is strong, there is less freedom to make mistakes and less willingness to "own" them once they are made. All trainers have this need to some extent and, at times, feel threatened when their competencies are challenged. When these feelings of threat are experienced, "competent" trainers will accept them as real without acting on them, thus keeping their focus on the group rather than turning it inward. Many trainers, in fact, will mention these feelings of threat in order to accept them and achieve closure on them.

A distinction also should be made between *content* and *process* (or method). Trainers who assume advocacy positions because of their biases concerning the content of the training or the issues to be dealt with are not making effective use of their resources. If trainers value the process that enables participants to surface, clarify, and examine *their* issues in terms of the consequences, they can utilize their resources in the direction of the participants' goals rather than the trainers' own needs. This does not

171

mean, however, that trainers should not acknowledge their own values when it is appropriate. Trainer competency is best evaluated in terms of the trainer's knowledge of self and the consequences of his or her behavior as well as the trainer's repertoire of techniques.

Although trainers must interact freely with the participants in order for the participants to get to know them, the trainers are not always completely free to be themselves. For example, a trainer may have some curiosity about a personal, back-home problem of a participant but will not ask about it in the group. To do so could establish a norm for exploration of back-home personal problems, and the participants may perceive that it is all right to probe in these areas.

Equally important is the extent to which the trainers' behaviors are congruent with their stated values and espoused ethics. The management philosophy of the trainers should exemplify the democratic process, in staff-participant relationships and also among staff members themselves.

One way to implement the norm of equality and responsibility in the workshop is to maintain an atmosphere of informality between the participants and the staff. In general sessions, during informal discussions, staff members should feel free to disagree with one another and to air workshop problems, encouraging suggestions for solutions from the participants. Informality and openness are means by which to reduce the barriers of authority and to encourage the perception of staff members as resources rather than as experts.

Trainer Competency

Experiential activities and interventions can have powerful effects on participants and on what they do or do not learn. Thus, any intervention should be evaluated in terms of its effectiveness in facilitating a particular process or highlighting a significant learning event. Interventions should not be considered ends in themselves and should not be imposed on participants without adequate justification or rationale. Trainers are not employed to demonstrate their "bags of tricks."

The most critical element in experiential learning—or in any intervention—is the trainer; his or her experience, competency, openness, trustworthiness, and ethics provide a standard against which participants can model themselves or react. A trainer, therefore, should have a solid background in the behavioral sciences, particularly as they relate to personal, interpersonal, group, and organizational theory and practice. It is also important that trainers be strong in process skills and in the use of experiential interventions and that they have some background in and familiarity with personality theory and behavior pathology—to understand better what is happening with the individuals in the group. Of course, a competent trainer will acknowledge and accept his or her limitations; a course in behavior pathology or personality theory does *not* make a trainer a clinician.

Besides a relevant educational background, completion of an internship with the National Training Laboratories, University Associates, or their equivalent would be desirable.

Ethical Considerations in Design[1]

Ethical considerations in design are not a set of moral prescriptions superimposed on the learning process. They are not an intrinsic part of the success of the learning process; they protect the integrity of the participants and provide the climate in which participants can build trust and drop those defenses that inhibit learning.

Ethical considerations in design are vital not only professionally and philosophically, but also practically. A design that violates the training organization's espoused ethical considerations rarely works because it creates distrust on the part of the participants. A structured experience, for example, is a powerful vehicle for controlling and structuring the setting and the interpersonal environment of the participants. This control can be seen as manipulation, if it is not obvious that the design has some positive purpose. Its value is derived from its ability to teach by isolating and highlighting an issue in human affairs, so that this isolation facilitates learning and deepens understanding of the complex issue. Thus, while the activity itself is artificial, the experience that

---

[1]Much of the first half of this chapter was adapted from materials written by Joyce Paris for the TIGER handbook.

occurs during the activity is real. The problem is that one may become overly interested or invested in a design (either a specific exercise or a total workshop) and confuse this relationship to the extent that the design becomes the important reality. There is a great danger that such overemphasis on one's techniques can obscure the workshop's goals and the participants' needs.

Data-Based Interventions Versus "Intuition"

In training groups, a considerable amount of time is spent by both the trainer and the participant in observing the interactions of others, observing one's own reactions and feelings as they occur, and observing the processes of the group as a whole. These observations are the data on which interventions and feedback are based. The more frequently one observes an event, the more secure one feels in intervening in or giving feedback about that event. In addition, other group members observing the same events can validate or question an individual's perceptions of those events.

Interventions that do not appear to be based on data generated by the group can be described as "intuitive" interventions. When asked where he or she obtained information, an "intuitive" intervenor may respond, "I have a gut feeling about it" or "I'm getting these vibes." Most of these kinds of interventions may be pure projection. (Much feedback, even when data based, is partially founded in projection; otherwise the observer might not have noticed or been attuned to the particular behavior.) In any event, it is important to ascertain where the information is coming from. When it is based on events in the group, it is important that those events be described as support for the feedback. When the intervention or feedback is "intuitive," it is important to state that the information is coming from the giver and that it may or may not be related to the receiver. Unfortunately, some trainers or group members identify with their intuitions and are unwilling to make this distinction.

Interpretation, like intuition, also comes from the giver. Interpretations are ways of perceiving reality that are based on some theory. The theory may be a system devised by other people (e.g., psychoanalytic theory) or it may be one's own theory. Theory is a way of constructing or explaining reality so that it makes sense to some people. It is not reality in itself. The interpretations in the giver's head may or may not be relevant to the behavior or theory of the receiver. Although it is almost impossible to never interpret the behavior of other people, one can keep those interpretations to oneself and relate to the other individuals in a more direct way. If an interpretation is made, it is important to acknowledge that it is an interpretation and not an observation and that the ownership lies strictly with the giver. Sometimes individuals are so enthralled with their interpretations that they are unwilling to give them up. In these instances, they may either question the recipients in ways that confirm their interpretations or literally push the recipients to accept the interpretations.

Helping the Participants to Process Their Learnings

A frequent occurrence in a training workshop is participant failure in a task, or at least failure to perform well on a task, because the workshop is designed to shake up some myths about how easy it is to be effective in one's relationships with people. People often learn more from their failures than from their successes, albeit a little more uncomfortably. Most people can weather task failure if what is exposed is the error of their assumptions about interpersonal issues, rather than their lack of intelligence or worth. Trainers need to be conscious of this distinction and use their skills to help participants process the experience of failure.

The average participant is naturally somewhat apprehensive about entering a workshop culture in which the rules and norms may be different from what the participant is used to. The participant's anxiety is further heightened as he or she perceives that the group members will be involved in activities for which the outcome is uncertain. The trainer should remember the vulnerability of this position and help the participants to work through their natural apprehensions until they adapt to the norms of the training event.

Processing Time. Time must be allowed for the participants to diagnose and discuss their experiences and elicit learnings generated by the design and then to debrief and work through feelings engendered by the experience. Processing time often is unintentionally abbreviated by trainers who have a tendency to crowd a workshop schedule in their eagerness to provide a rich experience. However, taking the time to process the participants' experiences is the *basic design element* of experiential learning. Too many activities in too little time results in an overload of unprocessed data and consequential confusion on the part of the participants. The commitment to look at the process is the key to experiential learning. Unless there is time to assimilate and understand an experience, there is little value in going through the experience itself. As noted previously, the effective use of processing time also allows a participant to deal better with perceived errors or failures and to create learnings and a sense of success out of such experiences.

The need to allow processing time is related to the need to allow enough small-group time. The small group may be instructed to process a task or may be free to develop its own path to effectiveness as a learning unit. The internal development of the small group is organic and not directly subject to the workshop design. However, the design that abbreviates small-group time—or does not place it strategically—mitigates the potential for learning in the workshop.

Risk Level

An important dimension of any design is its risk or level of potential threat, which usually is a function of perceived self-exposure. The risk level of a particular activity can be gauged by putting oneself in the participants' shoes and imagining oneself going through the activity or, better yet, by actually participating in the activity prior to the workshop. If participants can view the risk factor of an experience not in terms of how much they may lose but in terms of how much they may learn, they are better able to balance the risks against the gains in their own minds and make the decision to participate. A low-risk design that generates nothing more serious than good-humored frustration can be used early in a workshop as a stepping stone leading to more complicated processes. It is crucial that any feelings of embarrassment or exposure experienced by the participants at this stage be dealt with in a positive way.

It would be a mistake to identify the learnings from an experience as consistently tied to the risk level. Learning depends on a variety of factors, such as the readiness of the participants, the relevance of the design to the goals of the workshop, the sequencing of other experiences, and the imaginativeness of the design itself. In general, activities based on affect-laden issues such as personal competence, power, and feedback are more risky than those that relate to group-level data and for which individual responses are not identified or sharing is optional. Generally, high-risk activities are best reserved for small groups within a workshop. Participants usually have a greater level of trust within their own group than they do within the total community.

There is a tendency among some trainers to select all low-risk experiences and to underestimate the strength of the participants. Unfortunately, if no risk is taken, much of the power of experiential learning is lost. For example, giving and receiving personal feedback always involves discomfort as well as excitement. If one wishes to avoid dealing with such risk, however, one might as well eschew experiential learning and choose an alternative learning model.

An effective training design represents consideration of the ethical issues that foster a nondefensive learning environment and is structured to most effectively and clearly guide an educational experience within that environment. As the trainer's understanding and repertoire of structural interventions increase, he or she will be better able to adapt old interventions to here-and-now needs of the group and to design new interventions that are appropriate to the goals of the particular training experience. Design is not an isolated skill in training; it is fundamental to both the understanding of the training and the provision of a meaningful educational experience.

Group Ownership of Its Own Data

Respect for the privacy of information generated within a group (or subgroup) increases the likelihood that members will "open up" in their interactions within the group. This does not mean that a group may not willingly decide to share with the larger community some information about itself; but such information usually is limited to comments about group processes (how the group is working) and does not include content (what and who the group is talking about). There is also a great deal of difference between having the group be reported on by outsiders and allowing the group members to volunteer information in their own words and style.

In one intervention activity, group A (the consultant group) observed group B (the client group) and diagnosed the issues that were blocking movement in group B. Group A then designed a plan to facilitate group B's growth and presented it to group B. The groups' roles were then reversed and because each group in the workshop played both the designer and the client roles, the principle of equal vulnerability was maintained. However, during the intervention, three things became apparent: (a) the diagnoses of the groups' issues were generally astute and accurate; (b) the designed interventions were often creative and potentially helpful; and (c) the intergroup anger and resistance generated by the intervention lingered throughout the rest of the workshop. In a modified version of the activity, each group was charged with diagnosing itself and then presenting its self-diagnosis on an important issue to the consulting group and *asking* for assistance. There was great improvement in both groups' willingness to accept help nondefensively on the issues that the group members had decided was important to them.

DESIGNING INTERVENTIONS FOR EXPERIENTIAL LEARNING

Design skills are necessary to create new learning activities, select established ones, or integrate several in planning a complete workshop. Not all new trainers express an interest in creating new learning experiences, but they still must select activities and exercises to implement their training goals. Furthermore, as their competency in this role develops, their interest in and need to create new experiences will probably also develop, since one's confidence in selecting the most appropriate intervention is based on one's awareness of design considerations. Creating new experiences and modifying old ones are necessary not only to make the experiences relevant and sequentially meaningful, but also to insure involvement in and commitment to the design by the training staff. The principles of design discussed here will apply to both activities and total workshop experiences; some specific references to special workshop issues will be found later in this chapter.

Structural Considerations in Design

Goals

The goal of the training experience is the first structural consideration (see also Pfeiffer & Jones, 1973). When the participants have experienced the intervention, they should have had a chance to learn something about the issues related to its goal. Considering these issues is also the first step in building a new activity. For example, in designing an activity with the goal of learning something about the ramifications of competitiveness between groups, the first step is to decide under what conditions the groups will compete with one another. The first step, however, is not the most difficult part of designing. The difficult part is to design an activity that the participants can *manage* within the workshop setting. "Manage" refers not only to time and available resources but also to the level of readiness of the participants, i.e., whether they can profit from an experiential intervention.

A learning design should have enough interest to create excitement but not be so loaded that it also creates confusion or chaos. If too much happens, it becomes impossible for the participants to track and process the experience. It is helpful to pretest a new design on a practice group when such a group is available. The alternative is to make some sensitive, educated guesses about how people are likely to react to the design in a laboratory setting and then to discuss the design idea with another trainer who has no investment in the design and can serve effectively as a "devil's advocate."

Sometimes a structured activity that has a deceptive element may be used to facilitate a learning goal. For example, a role-play situation in which some participants are unaware of the roles played by others might be used to highlight listening skills or leadership styles. This type of "manipulation," even though it may be fun, can create distrust of the trainers on the part of some participants. The choice to use such activities must be weighed in terms of the learning payoff versus the risk of creating distrust, which then must be surfaced and dealt with.

Content

Much effective experiential learning is based on the content of the participants' back-home situations or simulations of such situations. This lends greater credibility to the task. However, back-home content does not always relate to the issues one is attempting to surface. It also may be "too close to home," so that participants could become tangled up in intense affective issues that block new learning. Activities that do not include back-home content, while they may appear less relevant, have the advantage of freeing the participants from prior knowledge and roles so that fresher views of such things as their behavioral styles or other critical issues can surfaced with a variety of non-content-specific activities. The job communication, and membership-leadership styles can easily be surfaced with a variety of non-content, specific activities. The job of the trainer is to seek a balance between emotionally involving content and more "distant," more easily examined content. Content-based activities can be more functional during the latter part of a workshop to aid the participants in applying their new learnings to their back-home situations.

Participant Involvement

A good design utilizes the largest number of participants in an active learning situation. If the design creates a number of inactive participants, it should be modified to give them specific observation tasks or other tasks that will keep them busy and allow them to participate in the final discussion of the activity.

Clarity and Simplicity

A good design is basically simple; a design becomes ineffectual when there is a lack of clarity or ability to retrieve and process what happened. Frequently, designs are ineffectual because they are too complicated. An effective design can be a one-line question or a simple rule to guide discussion (e.g., paraphrasing). It is important to remember that experiential learning involves *feelings* as well as ideas, and even the most intelligent participant will walk around slightly clouded at times. If a design must be complicated, its tracking mechanisms (rating sheets, graphs, etc.) must be clearly defined and able to be interpreted. Additional staff members also may be needed to implement such a design.

The need for clarity also applies to the instructions for an activity. Participants who are "stirred up" or fatigued can become confused about even the most simple instructions. In a workshop setting, people are least interested in learning how to follow instructions, so their instructions need to be clearer than in other settings. The use of newsprint or printed handouts to supplement verbal instructions generally is desirable. Confusing instructions may increase the natural resistance to participation and may result in irritation and anger, with the result being that the potential value of the experience is lost.

Structured Versus Unstructured Experiences

Trainers may have biases about how much structure should be included in a workshop. These biases range from almost no structure (all unstructured group time) to complete structure (no unstructured group time). The issues of how much structure is to be built into the design and whether or not to have trainers in each group will be dependent on the sophistication of the participants, the availability of staff, the goals of the workshop, etc. The question of structure is probably more a function of trainer preference than of actual effect on learning. Some differences between the two types of designs follow.

A structured workshop consists of a series of inputs and experiences, one building on the other, in which participants are asked to perform certain tasks and to examine the resulting interactions in terms of the feelings, attitudes, perceptions, insights, and concepts that were generated. For example, an activity in which one group observes another group working and feeds in process observations is a commonly used structured experience. Time also is provided for unstructured group sessions to *process* each structured intervention: to look at content issues, share reactions, discuss patterns and dynamics, develop principles, and plan how to apply the learnings (see also Pfeiffer & Jones, 1980).

In less structured workshops, most of the time is spent in unstructured groups, with a trainer present during group time. In these groups there are no agenda, no set tasks or procedures, and no direction specified by the trainer. From this unstructured and often chaotic beginning, group members attempt to build a cohesive learning unit in which most of what they learn is generated by their own activities and interactions. The group meetings are interspersed with some structured activities such as theory sessions, community exercises, and other kinds of groupings with specified tasks. The major block of time, however, is occupied by the unstructured groups.

In addition to the degree of formal structure, there are other differences between structured and unstructured training groups (for a discussion of the merits and uses of each, see also Boshear, 1976, and Gibb, 1976):

1. The learning goals of the structured workshop tend to be more specific and the structured interventions guide participants toward them. These training events usually have a content focus, e.g., leadership development, team building, or assertion training, and more time is spent in developing conceptual understanding and individual and group skills.

2. There is much less guidance in an unstructured workshop; this design is used more when greater awareness of self or of interpersonal processes is the goal of the event. It is often "exploratory," and much of the learning is generated by the participants' discoveries about themselves and themselves in relation to other people.

3. Structured workshops generally are less anxiety provoking, since the structure itself tends to provide an anchorage.

4. The unstructured group is more free-flowing, and anxiety is produced as members attempt to organize and direct themselves. This anxiety then becomes part of the learning experience.

5. Feedback usually is more systematic in a structured design and frequently is in the form of self-scored inventories or instruments that measure specific characteristics or attitudes. These instruments usually are based on action-research models, and many of the scoring procedures have action implications.

6. Feedback in the unstructured group usually is interpersonal and generally is based on perceptions that the members have of one another and of their behaviors.

Through the use of trainerless or self-directed groups within structured workshops, a large number of participants (e.g., forty to sixty) can participate with fewer staff members (e.g., one or two).

In groups in which the members have been working together for some time, these differences become obscured and may even shift. That is, the members may become much more comfortable with, or "hooked on," the unstructured sessions and resist (or even rebel against) a task when it is imposed on them. Important dynamics can be learned, however, when an ongoing training group is forced to mobilize its resources to accomplish a structured task. New leadership patterns may emerge as the group is called on to surface or return to the less valued task-oriented skills at a time when the premium is on socio-emotional skills. At this time the trainer can point out that both task and maintenance functions need to be present for the group to be well-balanced, rather than one skill being valued to the exclusion of the other.

The Design Task and the Training Staff

The training staff should begin to design a workshop with a general discussion of the goals of the event. Included in this discussion would be some educated guesses about the learning expectations of the participants, their levels of motivation, and their knowledge or understanding of experiential learning and human relations training. Sometimes an assessment of participants' needs can be collected from them prior to the workshop; these needs then can be evaluated and incorporated into the training design.

If the initial discussion runs on for some time, it may become obvious that a competent trainer could design the workshop in a fraction of the time that it takes the total staff to do it. The larger the staff, the stronger is this temptation. But proceeding by oneself not only eliminates the resources of the other staff members, it almost guarantees their half-hearted performance in the workshop. People support decisions that they are involved in, especially when those decisions involve public performance. In addition, one of the main purposes of designing with a staff is to build staff relationships. A good team relationship in staff planning makes a great difference in how a workshop is run.

When a discussion of the goals of and nature of the participants in a workshop becomes redundant, it is helpful to change the subject and to chart the designated lunch and coffee breaks for the workshop on newsprint. If this move is greeted with obvious relief by the group, the members are ready to move on in their planning.

The next decision may be the nature, size, and approximate amount of time to be spent in small groups. At this point, it may be helpful to consider all the opportunities for participants to interact with each other in the total community group and, at the same time, to retain the potential of these interactions to be meaningful. In addition to the community group and ongoing small groups, a workshop may include some experiences in subgroups, cross-group pairings, or other variations.

Once the arrangement of participants is tentatively settled, the consideration of the *flow* of the design is the next step. Not only does the content of what is being taught have a flow or build on itself, but the actual movement within the workshop should have the variety and balance to facilitate learning.

When the design group has finished revising and consolidating the design (this may take several sessions), it probably will be tempted to use the design for all future training events, handing it neatly typed to any new staff members. Unfortunately, this rarely works; the energy and team effort (ownership) that go into creating or remodeling a design are evidenced in its presentation, and these would be missing if other persons attempted to implement the design in a workshop.

One of the last steps in planning a design is to assign responsibility for implementing it to various staff members. It is wise to share the implementation by utilizing unique individual resources. It is also prudent to be wary of any staff member who disclaims a need for up-front performance and relinquishes this opportunity for leadership in the workshop. There may be a tendency for such a person to develop a late-blooming anger about his or her role (or lack of one) in the workshop.

Methods and Criteria for Judging the Outcomes of a Design

The method for judging whether or not the outcomes of a design were as planned may be simple, such as a process discussion or a diagnosis of what happened, or may include an evaluation tool or success measure. For example, the outcome of an experience in communication may be a discussion about the difficulties of speaking and listening accurately. In a data-based activity, the outcome is judged from the data generated by the experience itself.

The criteria for judging the outcome of a design are not easy to devise or anticipate and often are overlooked. For example, a group of trainers had the task of designing an activity to illustrate group cooperation and productivity. They identified some of the conditions that create group solidarity and productivity, such as common threat from the outside, a pressure or urgency to complete the task, or a strong identification bond within the group. The trainers then gave the participants the following task:

> Your task is to respond to a threat from your central office [a telegram was read] to cut off all funds and support. You have one-half hour to decide how to deal with this threat.

With great zeal and productivity, the participants went about finding a way (a written counterproposal and action plan) to forestall the threat. When the half-hour was up, the group had produced a proposal, but the trainers had no real method or criteria for judging the outcome of the activity or for measuring success. As a consequence, what started with a fine beginning ended somewhat lamely with a humorous intervention (a mock figure from the central office). The trainers did, however, follow the activity with a lecturette about the conditions that create group cooperation. What was a good demonstration could have been a better experience if it had included a method for judging the outcome of the design. A simple vote by participants on whether or not cooperation existed and whether or not an effective counterproposal was produced would have allowed the participants to better process and understand their experience and to improve their performance. The *method* in this case would be the vote (self-perception). The *criteria* would be the percentage of members that experienced learning.

In summary, it may be helpful to look at how a simple activity can fulfill all the structural components in a design and also, by changing one element, can have an entirely different outcome.

The Flying Object

Working within small groups, the participants have the task of building a flying object. They have one hour in which to complete this task. Each of four groups will produce approximately one-fourth of the final product. It is suggested that the groups use the first fifteen minutes to work together to design the object and assign the responsibility for producing parts of the object to each group. During the production time, although each group will work in a different room, the members may wander freely from group to group to check and revise their work.

Goals: 1. Explore group and intergroup cooperation.
   2. Produce an object that flies.

Related Issues: Interdependence for success; common purpose; task and goal defined; and open, free communication set up.

Content: Production is real, the product unreal.

Participant Involvement: Everyone.

Clarity and Simplicity: High.

Method for Judging the Attainment of Goal #1:   Ask people to rate how much they experienced a sense of community and intergroup cooperation.

Method for Judging the Attainment of Goal #2:   Try to make the object fly.

Criteria for Attaining Goal #1:   People report a high sense of community and intergroup cooperation.

Criteria for Attaining Goal #2:   The object flies.

In order to change this activity into one that guarantees failure (the object does not fly and people do not experience feelings of community or cooperation) and to illustrate the importance of issues related to the goals, the trainers could omit the instructions establishing the norm of open communication across groups (the groups probably never will get out of the planning stage). A formal, rigid manner of communication also could be established, e.g., "During 'work' time you may not communicate with other groups except through an appointed representative. If you feel that this person is not being an effective communicator, you may select another representative, but you may have only one representative in another production group at one time." Establishing these arbitrary communication modes—which are not foreign to some organizations—almost guarantees that the object will never get off the ground in the allotted time. The processing of this activity obviously would have quite a different focus from the processing of the first variation.

DESIGNING WORKSHOPS FOR EXPERIENTIAL LEARNING

Factors To Be Considered

The nature of training to be accomplished in a workshop is only one of a number of factors that must be assessed by the training staff before a description of the program is offered to potential participants and before the design of the workshop is created.

This discussion will be concerned with the design of three levels of training workshops. The basic workshop is complete unto itself. The intermediate and advanced workshops have as their prerequisites the basic workshop or equivalent experience. Although the advanced workshop does not necessarily depend on the intermediate workshop, the intermediate or equivalent experience is highly desirable. During the progression from basic to advanced workshops, the participants are given more responsibility for influencing, and finally planning, much of their own learning. The workshops used as examples here deal primarily with training and consultation skills rather than with personal growth because the primary goals of the former center around *inter*personal learning and change. The format for outlining the learning goals and vehicles for implementing these goals will vary from the basic to the advanced workshop to illustrate different models for charting these activities. Nailing down learning goals and ways to implement them is not the most exciting part of the training staff's job, but the process and the product will provide logic and direction to the workshop activities.

Workshops designed for different purposes frequently contain elements in common. These elements generally represent a core of learnings that are prerequisites for other learnings in the workshop. In designing for a workshop the trainers need to ask "What skills and conceptual tools are needed by the participants to enable them to profit most from the potential learnings in this workshop?" For example, the learnings to be abstracted from an intergroup-conflict situation would be minimal if the participants did not have the conceptual background and process skills needed to "see" what was going on and thus take effective action to resolve the conflict. The emotions that can be aroused when participants feel exposed, vulnerable, or defensive frequently cloud their perceptions and decrease their ability to benefit from the situation in terms of learning. A background in participant-observer skills and concepts relevant to the issues at hand enable the participants to diffuse, objectify, and manage the interpersonal, group, or intergroup processes so that the inherent learnings become more available to them.

One element common to many designs is the development of communication skills. The skill to diagnose how a group or team is working is important if team members are to process how effectively the group is functioning and develop action plans for improving its effectiveness. Workshops that utilize groups as their primary learning unit will contain elements for studying small group behavior. Every workshop that has improving interpersonal effectiveness as one of its goals will include practice in giving and receiving *feedback*. Lastly, learning about one's own interpersonal or leadership style is relevant to a supervisory or management workshop as well as to basic, intermediate, or advanced human relations training.

Focus of the Workshop

The term "focus" here is similar to the term "goal" but is more related to the target toward which the workshop activities are aimed. For example, the goal of "increased awareness of self" could be achieved through a focus on the self in isolation, the self in interpersonal interactions or group processes, or the self in terms of leadership styles and organizational behavior. Different workshops in different settings may focus on different aspects of the same human interactions and may vary in the level of intensity through which the participants must work in order to achieve the potential learnings. Described below are three general foci with associated levels of intensity and some rationale for staff decisions concerning how the workshops will be conducted. These categories are meant to be suggestive and do not represent mutually exclusive events or staffing decisions. (For example, self-oriented programs need not be intensive and can be conducted with less affective and more intellectual emphasis.)

Intensive, self-oriented workshops. These experiences are centered around individuals' relationships to themselves and are *intra*personal in nature. The emphasis is on the personal growth of the individual and only secondarily on *inter*personal and group processes. This type of workshop may not utilize small groups as the basic learning unit (Weir, 1975) but may depend on total-community sharing sessions to process activities that the participants have worked on individually. As a consequence, the total number of participants may be limited to allow the training staff to keep track of individual progress and problems and to monitor the pace. Since these types of workshops tend to be intense and are more closely related to psychotherapy, the training staff ideally would contain at least one individual with a clinical background. These workshops generally are referred to as personal growth events.

Intensive, self-other, group-oriented workshops. The primary goal of these workshops is to provide an intensive group experience in which individuals learn not only about small-group behavior, but also about their own impact on the process and on individual group members. The focus is on *inter*personal interactions and small-group processes. The basic learning unit is the small group, with a trainer in each group to facilitate the learning process. Since this experience is intensive, the trainer will track individual movement (either forward or backward), monitor destructive interactions or norms, and support individuals who may be in danger of having their personal space or values violated. Basic human relations training and encounter groups fall into this category.

Extensive, leadership- and work-oriented workshops. If learning about leadership styles and how groups or teams function is the primary goal of the workshop, the training staff may decide to utilize self-directed groups as the basic learning unit in which group members process their own interactions and feedback system. To assist group members to conduct their own groups, the training staff may provide tools such as structured interventions, theory presentations, and instruments. If there are sufficient trainers, the staff may decide to put one in each group. The participants' learnings about group process may be used to provide a model through which to examine their back-home work groups. These workshops tend to be more structured than the previous ones, although ample unstructured time is provided in the small groups.

Type of Client

Experiential learning, in contrast to traditional learning methods, has a strong potential for reaching the emotional resources of the individual and for providing an intensive personal and group experience. Most prospective participants today have some awareness of such programs and, to some extent, self-select themselves into or out of programs on the basis of their own personal goals and what they perceive the intensity (threat) level of the experience to be. Individuals who seek an intensive group or personal experience would select the first two types of workshops. Individuals who want a more structured or skill-oriented learning experience would select the third type of workshop. On the other hand, many workshops are designed as part of an organizational training or change program in which the participants have little choice. In these situations the nature of the client system must be assessed in terms of the organizational culture and the types of experiences that are acceptable or not acceptable (seen as legitimate or not legitimate) in that culture. Thus, the imposition of an encounter-group format on a highly conservative, task-oriented population undoubtedly would have negative consequences. Even with conservative populations, however, the trainer can facilitate a considerable amount of learning about group process and leadership styles by providing more structure and theory and by explaining that the small groups will provide the vehicle through which these processes will be studied. Calling the small groups study groups, process groups, or learning groups helps participants to see the relevance of processing to learning goals. Once a structured experiential workshop is experienced, many participants may be ready for or want a more intensive group experience.

Stranger Versus Affiliation Groups

Stranger groups are composed of participants who have no previous history together, are meeting for the first time, and do not expect to have a continuing relationship after the workshop. Affiliation groups are composed of groups who do have a previous history together and will continue in some type of relationship after the workshop. There is less risk in providing an intense group experience (barring other contingencies such as emotionally unstable participants) for a stranger group than there is for an affiliation group.

One reason for this is that previously unresolved conflicts among participants who work together frequently are surfaced but not resolved during a workshop. Problem issues may be carried over into post-workshop relations, where the expertise to work them through is not present. In addition, participants may be reluctant to expose themselves in front of their colleagues or co-workers (many times legitimately so), and will strongly resist any attempts by the training staff to encourage them to be open and to exchange feedback. On the other hand, many intact groups may be ready, because of previous preparation, to benefit greatly from an intensive group experience (such as team building). In such groups, however, ongoing (follow-up) experiences with the trainer serve as a safe-guard.

In designing a training program to be conducted within an organization, the trainer should confer with a person in the organization to determine the assignment of participants to groups. For example, one might want to avoid putting people from the same work unit in the same group, particularly if there is a supervisor-subordinate (or, in another case, a husband-wife) relationship. Because such participants have a history and will continue in a relationship after the workshop, the level of risk taking and sharing within the small groups may be particularly difficult for them. It also is difficult for participants who know each other to parcel out behavior at the workshop as opposed to their behavior back home or on the job. In conducting feedback sessions with such mixes, the trainer should emphasize that the behavior to be rated or discussed is the behavior that occurs *during the workshop*. Examples of previous behavior may not be available to all participants within the group and are not valid subject matter unless they relate directly to the issue at hand.

Ratio of Staff to Participants

A major issue here is one of economics in terms of available staff and the expense of the workshop. In a workshop involving six groups, a T-group format requires a minimum of six staff members; the same number of self-directed groups can be conducted by two or three staff members (or even one highly qualified and highly energetic staff member). Although both formats can provide highly significant learnings, the self-directed groups do not provide the opportunity for an intense, personal relationship between the trainer and the group members.

The purpose of the workshop also may determine the staff-participant ratio. Some advanced training programs, such as personal growth, purposely involve the large community group in sharing and processing workshop activities. In these workshops, two or three staff members are needed to conduct the activities and to keep track of individual participant movement.

When the number of trainers and participants is very large (ten groups and ten trainers, for example) and the workshop design calls for a T-group format, it can be extremely difficult to design the program. Communicating and keeping track of information become difficult, and decison making becomes a nightmare. The problem can be solved by dividing the workshop in half, and running two laboratories with five staff members and five groups each.

Visibility and Availability of Trainers

Some attention should be paid to the *visibility* of (length and frequency of presentations made by) different staff members. Some trainers enjoy presenting theory and conducting activities; they may volunteer to take a disproportionate share of such responsibilities. Trainers who have some reservations about their competency in this area may willingly take less responsibility. The training staff should be aware that participants may evaluate a trainer who appears to assume less responsibility as being less competent or in a secondary role. In addition, a group may feel slighted if it is assigned an apparently "second-class" trainer. Training staffs should ensure that everyone has some visibility in the total group throughout the workshop and that such visibility at some time is in a leadership role rather than a supportive role.

There are two kinds of trainer *availability*. The first is to be available to participants who need special attention—whether it be information, clarification of some issue, or additional support—that they are not able to get from their groups. The staff responsibility here is to be available throughout the workshop for any reasonable requests from participants.

The second kind of availability refers to socializing with participants during unscheduled time, and different trainers have different points of view about this issue. Some trainers may start to socialize with group members early in the free time of the workshop; other trainers wait until the latter part of the workshop to make themselves more available. The latter course is suggested here, for several reasons. First, there is a strong tendency for group members to initiate or continue the group's activities when a trainer is present, even if all the group members are *not* present. Second, the participants have a valid need to talk about the trainer, and his or her presence is likely to inhibit this. Third, the staff members need time together, particularly during the early part of the workshop, to assess how things are going, to identify any potential problems, to make any needed changes in scheduled activities, to check for clarity about who is doing what (and when), to provide mutual support, and to continue to develop staff relations (team building). Attempting to schedule staff meetings around individual trainers' social activities creates difficulties over and above the normal stresses of conducting the workshop. During the latter part of the workshop, when participants have worked through many of their interpersonal and group issues with each other and with the trainers, and when staff members have their own issues and workshop problems pretty well in hand, increased contact during free time between trainers and their group members takes place in a more relaxed atmosphere.

Scheduling Interventions

In designing any workshop it is important to be sensitive to pacing, to graduate the structured interventions in terms of risk potential and timing, and to provide sufficient time to process each experience. Presenting a theory session is more effective when the participants have had some opportunity to experience and perhaps struggle with the issue. Group observations are more useful after a few meetings when group members have become more group-process oriented. In structured sessions it should be obvious why one intervention comes before another. For example, a theory presentation on feedback should be given before using the JoHari Window as a model for examining the members' openness in giving and receiving feedback. The trainer then does not have to backtrack in order to make the model meaningful. Finally, activities that have a hidden or deceptive element (such as that which frequently occurs in role playing different supervisory styles) should be conducted early in the workshop. When participants begin to know each other well later in the workshop, a role that is inconsistent with the role player's natural self will be detected more easily. In addition, the deceptive element may be resented by the participants because they have put a great deal of effort into developing an atmosphere of trust.

Much of the process learning from structured sessions can be facilitated in T-groups by the trainers. With self-directed groups, after structured interventions have been used to highlight issues, it is important to provide sufficient unstructured time for the group members to process their experiences.

Some trainers tend to pack too many structured activities (even though they may be appropriate to the goals of the workshop) into the schedule for fear of missing an important learning. Consequently, there is less time for processing, and events appear to crowd each other in the schedule. Participants and staff members then feel rushed.

Small Work Groups

Experiential learning is best accomplished through the use of small work groups as the basic learning units through which workshop events are processed. Small groups provide maximum opportunity for individual participation, study of group phenomena, interpersonal feedback, and intergroup relations. Participants also experience a greater sense of involvement and responsibility for what they learn than they do when exposed only to large-audience or classroom-learning situations. The number and size of the small groups depend on several factors. Large work groups (twelve to fourteen members) take more time to accomplish tasks. They also provide less "air time" for each member and more room to "hide." If the workshop is short (one week or less), it usually is more effective to have a larger number of smaller groups (six to eight members). With self-directed groups, increasing the number of groups presents no problem; with T-groups, more groups may require more staff members.

If the groups are too small (four to five members), there may be too much air time available for each member, and the members may run out of steam. Members then may engage in bull sessions to fill up the time. They also may feel more vulnerable, with less room to hide. Participants need time to retreat and recoup after having been involved in an intensive interaction. Very small groups make this, and the process of moving in and out, more difficult. In addition, small groups may complete tasks or reach decisions too quickly, providing less data to process.

When possible, it is better to have an even number of groups than an odd number. Groups can then be paired off for activities such as group-on-group observations. An odd number of groups requires a type of round-robin schedule, which takes more time. For example:

Three Groups	Four Groups
40 minutes: A observes B (C out)	40 minutes: $\begin{cases} \text{(A observes B)} \\ \text{(C observes D)} \end{cases}$
40 minutes: C observes A (B out)	
40 minutes: B observes C (A out)	40 minutes: Reverse groups

If the workshop has seven or more groups, it probably will be necessary to divide the workshop into two units, as discussed previously.

Groups Working with Other Groups

A source of rich learning in a workshop setting is tapped when ongoing (intact) groups work with one another. This provides each group with an opportunity to observe another group working and to obtain a more objective perspective on some of the dynamics that are operating. When their observations are not influenced by their own involvement, the observers gain insights into how their own group is handling similar issues.

Members also can obtain some valuable information from "outsiders." In addition, groups can be used as consultants to one another in order to experience the process of group diagnosis and intervention. The consultant/client pairing of groups increases the intention of each group to be more observant and to consider more carefully the relevancy and impact of any intervention it designs. Increased excitement also accompanies this kind of risk taking. Another area of learning that cannot be obtained when groups work separately deals with intergroup dynamics surrounding the issues of conflict, competition, and cooperation. Learnings from intergroup issues have broad applications to society in general, in which all kinds of groups interface on problems in ways that prevent mutual understanding and cooperation.

Group-on-Group Observations can be used to give groups an idea of how all groups develop, the levels at which they operate, and to what extent each of the groups involved has progressed in terms of dealing with and resolving its developmental issues.

Cross-Group Diagnoses and Interventions usually are reserved for advanced training workshops in which the participants' goals are to gain in-depth understanding of group dynamics and practice in diagnosing groups and planning interventions around diagnostic issues. Group members also learn from the experience of being diagnosed and from the final evaluation process (whether or not the intervention achieved its desired effect).

It is important to stress that an intervention that fails does not constitute a loss for either group. The potential for learning in such a case is frequently greater than when an intervention is successful, because a successful intervention leaves both groups with little inclination to process the event. The unsuccessful intervention generates energy (i.e., tension, a lack of closure) that can be productively reduced through processing. The problem here is to get both groups to work through the defensiveness that an ineffective intervention generates. Once this is accomplished, productive learning can take place.

Intergroup Conflict, Competition, and Cooperation can easily be studied in the experiential workshop with its multiple groups. In the course of any workshop, one can see intergroup stereotyping and competition arise naturally as a consequence of groups being exposed to each other and working on issues that are common to the workshop community (Bell, Cleveland, Hanson, & O'Connell, 1969; Blake, Mouton, & Sloma, 1965; Ermalinski, Hanson, & O'Connell, 1972). Groups quickly obtain labels such as "the fast group," "the serious group," "the happy group," "the late group," or "the slow group." Feelings of competition frequently occur when one group is observing another group and providing that group with feedback about how it is functioning. Under these conditions, the observed group will frequently react defensively to the observations made by the observing group. These intergroup dynamics are a reflection (albeit in attenuated form) of the dynamics that occur in back-home groups when the norms, standards, values, or goals of these groups are in conflict with those of other groups (e.g., labor/management, black/white, night shift/day shift). If the conditions that create tensions between groups are not reduced or resolved, the groups may become locked into mutually destructive interactions. Under conditions of intergroup conflict, some of the following conditions may occur:

1. Each group forms negative stereotypes of the other group. Communication is filtered through these stereotypes and may further distort each group's perceptions of the other.

2. Communication decreases or is censored because (a) members of one group do not want to see or hear the other group's point of view, but hear only that which supports their own position; (b) members see and hear only the differences and ignore the similarities between the groups' points of view; or (c) reasonable requests from the other group are heard as demands.

3. Hostility between groups increases; each begins to see the other group as antagonistic.

4. The groups withhold resources from each other. The resulting products are not as good or as creative as if the groups were to share or pool their resources.

5. The groups develop win-lose strategies; energy, creativity, and resources are expended in trying to make the other group lose; feelings are generated that tend to feed and perpetuate nonproductive interactions.

6. Interaction may decrease. The two groups may withdraw from each other to standoff positions or to positions of peaceful coexistence and avoidance of conflict at any cost.

In any effort to resolve intergroup conflict and move the groups in a direction of cooperation, trainers and group leaders can assist their groups to embark on a program of intergroup development that involves increasing communication and reducing the negative stereotypes that keep the groups divided. Some of the strategies for creating more constructive and cooperative intergroup relationships involve:

1. Helping each group to identify the conditions in its relationship with the other group that foster antagonism and nonproductive competition.

2. Helping each group to identify common goals, which provide an impetus for resolving intergroup problems.
3. Helping both groups to examine and understand their behavioral cultures.
4. Helping both groups to examine the stereotypes they have of each other and to reach a clear understanding of what they mean.
5. Helping each group to accept these stereotypes as "real" for the other group and to examine its own behaviors in light of these stereotypes to see to what extent these behaviors contribute to or perpetuate the stereotypes.
6. Developing action plans for identifying the key devisive issues, reducing them, and moving both groups in a cooperative direction.
7. Helping each group to understand that sharing and pooling resources rather than withholding them and channeling energy into cooperative efforts rather than draining them off into competitive struggles increases the energy levels of both groups and creates conditions that aid more creative problem solving.
8. Helping both groups to understand that intergroup relations, like team building, require continuous monitoring and checking, and developing a commitment from each group to this process.

Total-Group, Community, or Plenary Sessions

Sessions that involve the total participant population can be used in several ways to enhance the climate of the workshop and to provide learnings that are not readily obtainable in the small groups. One important function of the total-group session is to build a learning "community"—to enable participants from different groups to interact with one another and share experiences. Theory presentations frequently are made during these sessions to avoid duplication of staff activities and to provide a change of setting between the small group's activities and the conceptual material. The special setting enables the trainer to shift roles. General sessions also allow the total community to be exposed to staff members who have special skills or talents that participants in some of the small groups might otherwise miss. Finally, particular learning interactions such as intergroup dynamics can be processed with all groups present.

Physical Environment and Climate

The setting in which the workshop takes place is extremely important. Large auditoriums can create a sense of isolation and distance. Cramped quarters prevent movement and flexibility. An ideal setting would include one large room for general sessions and smaller rooms nearby for the work groups. The rooms should have adequate wall space to display taped-up newsprint posters. The community-session room should be large enough to allow all participants to move about and also to work privately in their small groups (by sitting together in small circles) without disturbing other groups. If possible each small-group room should have its own supplies such as an easel, newsprint, masking tape, and felt-tipped markers. Finally, all workshop rooms should be isolated from distractions such as outside people wandering in, outside noise, and telephone calls or other back-home intrusions. Obviously, the ideal setting will not always be available. Much preworkshop preparation involves locating sites where ideal conditions can be approximated and negotiating with sponsors and site managers for the best accommodations possible within the workshop budget.

The environment in which a workshop takes place can also influence feelings of safety and trust. The philosophy behind human relations training encourages experimentation and risk taking, and workshop participants frequently act and dress in ways that are not typical of their everyday life. Building a miniature society, a cultural island, with norms that are not consistent with the surrounding community might pose a threat to the participants' feelings of freedom regarding risk taking and experimentation. It is important, therefore, to be sensitive to the environment (hotel, small town, college campus, retreat houses, etc.) in which one plans to conduct a human relations training laboratory.

Part of the environmental support for participants in a workshop is the trainers themselves. In order for participants to express their feelings, opinions, and disagreements, a climate must be developed in which they feel relatively safe from evaluation, personal censure, and having their confidentiality violated. Trainers can facilitate this climate by being open themselves, by publishing ground rules concerning confidentiality, and by establishing and reinforcing a nonjudgmental and nonevaluative norm for the workshop. Human relations training also must model risk-taking behavior, expression and acceptance of both positive and negative feelings, and openness to receiving and giving feedback.

Materials and Handouts

Theory handouts are intended to relieve participants of the need to take notes during lecturettes so that they can focus on and react to what is being presented. The trainer may state that the handouts are not intended to be read during the oral presentation but are for the participants to read later. Generally, theory presentations can be kept short, with an outline format eliminating the need for detailed discussion on every point. Responsibility is shifted to the participants to abstract theory from their own interactions, with short oral theory presentations used to clarify or highlight pertinent issues.

Large pads of newsprint paper on easels, with felt-tipped markers, are better suited to illustrating points or making posters than are blackboards or overhead projectors. The material on newsprint sheets can be kept and posted about the room with masking tape. Subsequent presentations and activities then can be related to the material on the walls. Participants also can use newsprint in their groups to record items for the group's use or for presentation to the general session. Newsprint pads and easels are portable; they can be moved from place to place with ease.

Notebooks or folders can be provided to the participants to store handouts and other material such as the schedule of workshop activities, the goals of the workshop, or work-group rosters.

It often is useful to have a check list when gathering materials for a workshop. Aside from charts, easels, newsprint, and theory handouts, such items as name tags, felt-tipped markers, masking tape, pencils, blank paper, hole punches, and staplers are easy to overlook when packing for a workshop.

Dean's Report

Many training organizations will assign one person on the training staff as the dean of a workshop. In other organizations, the dean will be selected first and will then be given the responsibility for choosing his or her staff. The duties of the dean overlap those of the other staff members and consist of: (a) selecting the staff, (b) assuming administrative duties for the workshop; (c) conducting a training group, (d) meeting with other deans (if there are a number of workshops running concurrently) to coordinate activities of the overall learning community, and (e) writing the dean's report after the workshop is completed.

The dean's report can be useful to the staff and the organization for future reference and may include such items as:

1. A general description or outline of the workshop design, with a more detailed description of any unusual or experimental elements.
2. An evaluation of the elements in the workshop, from both the participants' and the staff's point of view, plus an evaluation of the workshop as a whole.
3. Modifications or changes that the staff would make based on the evaluations and their impressions.
4. An evaluation of the site, e.g., administrative support, meals, living accommodations, meetings rooms, and any other physical or service assets or liabilities.
5. Documentation and follow-up of any unusual incidents or problems concerning participants.

Ideally, the dean's report will be compiled in cooperation with the staff, prior to leaving the workshop site, when reactions, impressions, and descriptions of events are fresh. The report can be documented by the dean, organized, and typed later. Copies of the finished report generally will be distributed to the staff.

If no one on the training staff is designated dean, it is still a useful activity to write a report of the workshop. The staff discussion and analysis of the workshop, the identification of individual and group issues, and the opportunity to exchange feedback are educational experiences in themselves. The process also provides a debriefing period for staff members themselves and allows them to complete unfinished business and incomplete experiences. Unfortunately, after the completion of a workshop, many staff members, like participants, are eager to be on their way. As a consequence, the post-workshop evaluation may be abbreviated or eliminated. Because it is an extremely important function, staff time should be scheduled for the post-workshop evaluation and debriefing session.

Basic Human Relations Training

The Participants

The workshop brochure should clearly spell out the workshop goals and training format to enable potential applicants to screen themselves before the training event. If a participant is going to have difficulty in a human relations training laboratory, the potential probably is highest during the first training experience.

As a rule, the educational and vocational backgrounds of participants in human relations training will be primarily in the helping professions, business, government, education, and religious communities. Their occupational levels usually will range from lower to upper management and from skilled to professional backgrounds. Exceptions to the typically middle-class workshop population are those in experiential learning events specifically aimed toward less affluent, less vocationally skilled, frequently disenfranchised, and increasingly vocal members of the community. The democratic philosophy of human relations training mandates that training organizations take a proactive stance toward reaching into the community to make consultation and training available.

Groups within the training laboratory ideally will represent a mix along the dimensions of sex, age, race, and occupation. If there are only one or two members of a particular minority group, the staff may want to place them in the same group for mutual support; if there is only one minority-group member, that person may be placed in the group of a trainer of the same minority. When considering the diversity of potential applicants, it is important to consider whether members of the training staff represent that diversity. It would be somewhat foolish, for example, to work with a large number of black or female participants with no black or female staff member. A mixed staff keeps members sensitive to the special issues of the participants and can increase the awareness of personal biases within each trainer.

Workshop Goals

When planning a workshop, it is helpful to develop a list of possible interventions relevant to the learning goals described in the brochure. Sample skill areas and learning goals follow, with possible vehicles for implementing the goals. The activities and theory listed under "vehicle" are not all-inclusive, but are illustrative of many used in basic human relations training workshops. One vehicle may implement more than one learning goal. Interventions should be kept in a subordinate position to learning goals. Their primary function is to implement learning goals through experiential events, with theory inputs to clarify learnings. Designing a workshop around "favorite" interventions can subvert the primary purpose of the training event.

I. Skill Area: Communication
   A. Learning Goals
      1. To explore problems of sending and receiving messages in face-to-face communication.
      2. To practice skills in communication.
      3. To demonstrate the interdependence of both participators in effective communication.
      4. To become acquainted with the process of giving and asking for information (particularly in personally sensitive areas) and how to do this more effectively.
   B. Sample Vehicles
      1. Small structured or unstructured groups, theory presentation on listening and attending, demonstration, group discussion, data feedback, and practice.
      2. *Exercises:* Listening and Attending, One-Way/Two-Way Communication, feedback sessions, both spontaneous and structured (instruments).

II. Skill Area: Group Dynamics, Diagnostic and Process Skills
   A. Learning Goals
      1. To develop an awareness and sensitivity to *how* groups work and the dimensions of group behavior that facilitate or block effective team work.
      2. To learn to give feedback to a group using group-level dimensions.

B. Sample Vehicles
   1. Small structured or unstructured groups, theory presentation on "What to Look for in Groups," demonstration and practice.
   2. *Exercises:* Group-on-Group Observation and Feedback, Observation Guide: What to Look for in Groups.

Intermediate Human Relations Training

The Participants

The intermediate training workshop is a skill-oriented program for people who want to develop competence in designing and implementing experiential learning programs or interventions in their back-home work settings. It is further designed to increase their understanding of theories of group dynamics and experiential learning.

The workshop's basic learning goals should be clearly described in the brochure or other preworkshop information, along with the prerequisite knowledge or equivalent experience needed. The information in the brochure should enable prospective applicants to assess their own readiness and to screen themselves in or out of the training event. In the case of an ongoing training program, the training staff can screen potential participants.

The applicants for an intermediate workshop probably will have more in common in terms of their occupational backgrounds and their motives for attending. They will consist primarily of management developers, in-house change agents, teachers, workshop leaders, consultants, conference planners, and professionals who use experiential learning in their work. Applicants also will be clearer about their expectations and better able to match workshop goals to their own learning needs. Because these people will have been through previous experiential learning events, they probably will be more vocal if their expectations are not met. For example, if the participants discern that the workshop is essentially a repetition of their previous training experiences, they may feel deceived by the trainers. The design of the workshop, therefore, should clearly reflect the learning goals described in the workshop brochure.

Workshop Goals

The intermediate workshop can be offered as a public laboratory in which the goals of the workshop are predetermined and described by the training organization, or it can be one phase in a training program, in which case the training staff would probably collect data about the training needs of the participants. If the target population is known, preworkshop data can be collected in which prospective participants describe their own training needs. These self-diagnoses or need assessments can be collated and used as guidelines for workshop goals. The training staff can then plan activities relevant to these goals. The training staff also may include goals that it feels are important, even if they are not represented in the participants' need assessments.

Even when the workshop goals are predetermined by the training organization, part of the design may be tailored to allow the participants to determine their own learning goals. The staff and the participants then collaborate in implementing these goals.

If the participant population's first training experience was in a more structured workshop utilizing self-directed D-groups, it might be useful to provide their intermediate experience in T-groups, which would present alternative models for group-process analysis and learning. The T-group also provides a more intensive personal-growth experience and enables the staff members to have more personal and first-hand experiences with the participants.

If the participants' previous experience was in T-groups, a D-group format would provide an opportunity for them to take more responsibility for the functioning of their own groups. Switching from a T-group model to a D-group format is more difficult because of participants' expectations of having "their own trainer." On the other hand, once having had the experience of conducting their own groups, D-group participants may then resist or compete with a trainer in a subsequent T-group experience. In any event, having both experiences provides richer learnings than being exposed to only one.

The following list is a sample of goals that were collated from a need-assessment survey by participants and used to design an intermediate workshop. The vehicles for implementing the goals were listed by the staff.

Goals	Vehicles

Group Diagnostic and Process Skills:

1. To increase awareness of and sensitivity to group issues and problems and to identify the dimensions of group behavior that facilitate or hinder movement toward achieving its learning goals.

2. To learn how to collect and organize data about group issues or problems.

3. To learn and use behavioral science concepts as a tool in observing and understanding groups.

1. Group observations.
2. Group diagnosis.
3. T-group or D-group.
4. Theory presentation.

Design Skills:

To design interventions relevant to the diagnosis and sensitive to the issues involved.

Groups paired in consultant/client relationships to practice sequence of observation-diagnosis-design-implement-feedback-evaluation.

Intervention Skills:

1. To prepare to implement the intervention (identify appropriate personal and material resources, methods for tracking and retrieving the data, etc.).

2. To practice executing an intervention.

1. T-groups or D-groups as design teams.
2. Staff as consultants.
3. Group-on-group intervention.

Evaluation of the Intervention:

1. Prepare report for feedback to client group on perceived effects.

2. Prepare report for feedback to consultant group on experienced effects.

Advanced Human Relations Training

The advanced workshop is designed primarily for people who are either in consultant/training roles in their own organizations or for those who consult/train with organizations as external change agents. The primary purposes of the workshop are to increase the participants' level of awareness of the consultation process and to provide the participants with "live" experience with clients. The skills to be learned include clarification of the consultant's and client's roles and clarification of the task.

The Participants

Brochures for public workshops will be geared toward people who are, or expect to be, involved with clients. These people generally will be managers, trainers, consultants, administrators, health-care professionals, and applied-social-science professionals. They should have had, as prerequisites to the workshop, basic human relations training, intermediate training, and/or equivalent experience. Thus, this population will be fairly sophisticated in the theory and practice of experiential learning and change agentry.

Workshop Goals

The progress from basic human relations training through intermediate training to an advanced (consultation-skills) workshop represents a gradual process of increased responsibility, by the participants, for meeting their own learning needs. Advanced participants can be given almost complete responsibility for assessing their own needs and for designing, planning, implementing, and evaluating elements of the workshop. A major consequence of this is the increased confidence of the participants in their professional roles.

If the goal of the workshop is to provide "live" consultation experience, the training staff must obtain clients from the surrounding community prior to the workshop. These clients must be scheduled into the workshop design.

An advanced training design might include the goals that follow. Some of the goals are similar to those listed for the intermediate workshop. At this level, however, participants take full responsibility for implementing the goals and the training staff assumes more of a consultant role.

Goals	Vehicles
Diagnostic, Design, and Implementation Skills:	
1. To continue to develop these skills with temporary groups, ongoing work teams, and larger organizational units.	1. Consultant/client teams; group-on-group interventions. 2. Process groups.
2. To learn ways to evaluate interventions and follow-up.	1. Live-client contact; consultant teams. 2. Design teams.
Client Contact:	
1. To provide experience with clients, including initial contact, assessing the client's needs, intervening, feedback, and follow-up. 2. To build a client-consultant relationship.	1. Live client consulting; ongoing throughout workshop. 2. Consultant teams. 3. Process groups.
Team Building:	
1. To provide an opportunity for consultant teams to contract, diagnose, and intervene on intact groups and to experience feedback and evaluation. 2. To compare team building with temporary groups versus team building with ongoing or permanent groups.	1. Consultant-client teams. 2. Live-client consulting. 3. Process groups.
Consultation Skills:	
1. To explore different theories of consulting and different styles of practice. 2. To examine methods of preparation for the professional consultant. 3. To become acquainted with and to examine ethics and values in consulting.	1. Theory-input presentations. 2. Process groups. 3. Design teams.

REFERENCES

Baker, R.R. *Planning for effective team functioning: A manual*. Houston, TX: Training & Measurement Systems, 1977. (Available from Philip G. Hanson, 5451 Lymbar Drive, Houston, TX 77096)

Beckhard, R. The confrontation meeting. *Harvard Business Review*, March-April 1967, *45*(2), 149-155.

Bell, R.L., Cleveland, S.E., Hanson, P.G., & O'Connell, W.E. Small group dialogue and discussion: An approach to police-community relationships. *The Journal of Criminal Law, Criminology and Police Science*, 1969, *60*(2), 242-246.

Blake, R.R., & Mouton, J.S. *Corporate excellence through grid organization development*. Houston, TX: Gulf, 1968.

Blake, R.R., Mouton, J.S., & Sloma, R.L. The union-management intergroup laboratory: Strategy for resolving intergroup conflict. *The Journal of Applied Behavioral Science*, 1965, *1*(1), 25-27.

Boshear, W.C. A case for structure. In J.E. Jones & J.W. Pfeiffer (Eds.), *Group & Organization Studies*, 1976, *1*(2), 134-135.

Dyer, W.G. *Team building: Issues and alternatives*. Reading, MA: Addison-Wesley, 1977.

Ermalinski, R., Hanson, P.G., & O'Connell, W.E. Toward resolution of a generation gap conflict on a psychiatric ward. *International Journal of Group Tensions*, 1976, *2*(2), 77-89.

Gibb, J.R. A case for nonstructure. In J.E. Jones & J.W. Pfeiffer (Eds.), *Group & Organization Studies*, June 1976, *1*(2), 135-137.

Jones, J.E. The sensing interview. In J.E. Jones & J.W. Pfeiffer (Eds.), *The 1973 annual handbook for group facilitators*. San Diego, CA: University Associates, 1973.

Pfeiffer, J.W., & Jones, J.E. Design considerations in laboratory education. In J.E. Jones & J.W. Pfeiffer (Eds.), *The 1973 annual handbook for group facilitators*. San Diego, CA: University Associates, 1973.

Pfeiffer, J.W., & Jones, J.E. Introduction to the structured experiences section. In J.W. Pfeiffer & J.E. Jones (Eds.), *The 1980 annual handbook for group facilitators*. San Diego, CA: University Associates, 1980.

Reilly, A.J., & Jones, J.E. Team-building. In J.W. Pfeiffer & J.E. Jones (Eds.), *The 1974 annual handbook for group facilitators*. San Diego, CA: University Associates, 1974.

Schein, E.H. *Process consultation: Its role in organizational development*. Reading, MA: Addison-Wesley, 1969.

Weir, J. The personal growth laboratory. In K.D. Benne, L.P. Bradford, J.R. Gibb, & R.O. Lippitt, *The laboratory method of changing and learning*. Palo Alto, CA: Science & Behavior Books, 1975.

SUGGESTED READINGS

Alban, B.T., & Pollitt, I.L. Team building. In T.H. Patten (Ed.), *OD: Emerging dimensions and concepts.* Madison, WI: Organization Development Division, American Society for Training and Development, 1973.

Beckhard, R. *Organization development—Strategies and models.* Reading, MA: Addison-Wesley, 1969.

Benne, K.D., Bradford, L.P., & Lippitt, R. The laboratory method. In L.P. Bradford, J.R. Gibb, & K.D. Benne (Eds.), *T-group theory and laboratory method.* New York: John Wiley, 1964.

Bennis, W.G. Goals and meta-goals of laboratory training. *Human Relations Training News,* Fall 1962, *6*(3), 1-4.

Bennis, W.G., Benne, K.D., & Chin, R. (Eds.). *The planning of change: Readings in the applied behavioral sciences.* New York: Holt, Rinehart and Winston, 1969.

Bennis, W.G., & Slater, P.E. *The temporary society.* New York: Harper & Row, 1968.

Blake, R.R., & Mouton, J.S. Power, people, and performance reviews. *Advanced Management,* 1961, *10*(4), 13-17.

Blake, R.R., Shepard, H.A., & Mouton, J.S. *Managing intergroup conflict in industry.* Houston, TX: Gulf, 1964.

Boone, T.A. Therapy or personal growth? In J.E. Jones & J.W. Pfeiffer (Eds.), *The 1975 annual handbook for group facilitators.* San Diego, CA: University Associates, 1975.

Bradford, L.P. (Ed.). *Group development* (Rev. ed.). San Diego, CA: University Associates, 1978.

Bradford, L.P. Creating a learning environment. In K.D. Benne, L.P. Bradford, J.R. Gibb, & R.O. Lippitt (Eds.), *The laboratory method of changing and learning: Theory and application.* Palo Alto, CA: Science & Behavior Books, 1975.

Burton, A. (Ed.). *Encounter: The theory and practice of encounter groups*. San Francisco: Jossey-Bass, 1970.

Chin, R. Evaluation research and documentation in programs using laboratory method. In K.D. Benne, L.P. Bradford, J.R. Gibb, & R.O. Lippitt, *The laboratory method of changing and learning*. Palo Alto, CA: Science & Behavior Books, 1975.

Drucker, P. *Managing for results*. New York: Harper & Row, 1965.

Dyer, W.G. (Ed.). *Modern theory and method in group training*. New York: Van Nostrand Reinhold, 1972.

Fordyce, J.K., & Weil. R. *Managing with people: A manager's handbook of organization development methods*. Reading, MA: Addison-Wesley, 1971.

French, J.R.P., Jr. A formal theory of social power. In D. Cartwright & A. Zander (Eds.), *Group dynamics, research and theory* (3rd ed.). New York: Harper & Row, 1968.

French, J.R.P., Jr., & Raven, B. The bases of social power. In D. Cartwright & A. Zander (Eds.), *Group dynamics, research and theory* (3rd ed.). New York: Harper & Row, 1968.

French, W.L., & Bell, C.H., Jr. *Organization development: Behavioral science interventions for organization improvement* (2nd ed.). Englewood Cliffs, NJ: Prentice-Hall, 1978.

Golembiewski, R.E., & Blumberg, A. (Eds.). *Sensitivity training and the laboratory approach: Readings about concepts and applications* (3rd ed.). Itasca, IL: F.E. Peacock, 1977.

Hanson, P.G., Baker, R., Paris, J., Brown-Burke, R., Ermalinski, R., & Dinardo, Q. *Training for individual and group effectiveness and resourcefulness*. Washington, D C : Veterans Administration Department of Medicine and Surgery, 1977.

Harrison, R. Research on human relations training: Design and interpretation. *Journal of Applied Behavioral Science*, 1971, 7 (1), 71-85.

Harvey, J. Some dynamics of intergroup competition. *Human Relations Training News*, Fall 1964-Winter 1964-65, 8(3 & 4), 1-7.

Havelock, R.G., & Havelock, M.C. *Training for change agents: A guide to the design of training programs in education and other fields*. Ann Arbor, MI: Institute for Social Research, 1973.

Jones, J.E., & Banet, A.J., Jr. Dealing with anger. In J.W. Pfeiffer & J.E. Jones (Eds.), *The 1976 annual handbook for group facilitators*. San Diego, CA: University Associates, 1976.

Kolb, D.A., Rubin, I.M., & McIntyre, J.M. *Organizational psychology: An experiential approach*. Englewood Cliffs, NJ: Prentice-Hall, 1971.

Lakin, M. *Interpersonal encounter: Theory and practice in sensitivity training*. New York: McGraw-Hill, 1972.

Lakin, M. Some ethical issues in sensitivity training. *American Psychologist*, 1969, 24(10), 923-928.

Lau, J.B. *Behavior in organizations: An experiential approach*. Homewood, IL: Richard D. Irwin, 1975.

Lewin, K. *Resolving social conflicts*. New York: Harper & Row, 1948.

Lieberman, M.A., Miles, M.B., & Yalom, I.D. *Encounter groups: First facts*. New York: Basic Books, 1973.

Likert, R. *The human organization: Its management and value*. New York: McGraw-Hill, 1967.

Lippitt, R.O., & Schindler-Rainman, E. Designing for participative learning and changing. In K.D. Benne, L.P. Bradford, J.R. Gibb, & R.O. Lippitt (Eds.), *The laboratory method of changing and learning: Theory and application*. Palo Alto, CA: Science & Behavior Books, 1975.

Luke, R., Jr., & Benne, K.D. Ethical issues and dilemmas in laboratory practice. In K.D. Benne, L.P. Bradford, J.R. Gibb, & R.O. Lippitt (Eds.), *The laboratory method of changing and learning: Theory and application*. Palo Alto, CA: Science & Behavior Books, 1975.

May, R. *Power and innocence: A search for the sources of violence*. New York: W.W. Norton, 1972.

Miller, D.C. *Handbook of research design and social measurement* (2nd ed.). New York: David McKay, 1970.

Napier, R.W., & Gersharfeld, M.K. *Groups: Theory and practice*. Boston, MA: Hougton Mifflin, 1973.

Nylen, D., Mitchell, J.R., & Stout, A. *Handbook of staff development and human relations training: Materials designed for use in Africa.* Arlington, VA: NTL Institute for Applied Behavioral Science, 1967. (Available only from Learning Resources Corporation, 8517 Production Avenue, P.O. Box 26240, San Diego, CA 92126)

Pfeiffer, J.W., & Jones, J.E. (Eds.). *A handbook of structured experiences for human relations training* (8 vols.). San Diego, CA: University Associates, 1969-1981.

Pfeiffer, J.W., & Jones, J.E. (Eds.). *The annual handbook for group facilitators* (10 vols.). San Diego, CA: University Associates, 1972-1981.

Porter, L., & Mill, C.R. (Eds.). *Reading book for human relations training.* Arlington, VA: NTL Institute for Applied Behavioral Science, 1976.

Ram Dass. *The only dance there is.* New York: Doubleday, 1974.

Robinson, J.P., Athanasiou, R., & Head, K.B. *Measures of occupational attitudes and occupational characteristics.* Ann Arbor, MI: Institute for Social Research, 1969.

Rogers, C. *Carl Rogers on encounter groups.* New York: Harper & Row, 1970.

Rogers, C. *On becoming a person: A therapist's view of psychotherapy.* Boston, MA: Hougton Mifflin, 1961.

Ryan, L.R. *Clinical interpretation of the FIRO-B.* Palo Alto, CA: Consulting Psychologists Press, 1971.

Schein, E.H., & Bennis, W.G. *Personal and organizational change through group methods: The laboratory approach.* New York: John Wiley, 1965.

Schutz, W.C. *FIRO: A three-dimensional theory of interpersonal behavior.* New York: Holt, Rinehart and Winston, 1958.

Schutz, W.C. *The interpersonal underworld.* Palo Alto, CA: Science & Behavior Books, 1966.

Seashore, E. What is sensitivity training? *NTL Institute News and Reports,* April 1968, 2(2).

Shaffer, J.B.P., & Galinsky, M.D. *Models of group therapy and sensitivity training.* Englewood Cliffs, NJ: Prentice-Hall, 1974.

Van Maanen, J. *The process of program evaluation: A guide for managers.* Washington, D C : National Training & Development Service Press, 1973.

Weschler, I., & Reisel, J. *Inside a sensitivity group.* Los Angeles: University of California Institute of Industrial Relations, 1960.

Weschler, I., & Schein, G.H. (Eds.). *Issues in human relations training.* Arlington, VA: National Training Laboratories (Selected Reading Series 5), 1962.

White, R., & Lippitt, R. Leader behavior and member reaction in three "social climates." In D. Cartwright & A. Zander (Eds.), *Group dynamics, research and theory* (3rd ed.). New York: Harper & Row, 1968.